# GO-TO FLIES

101 Patterns the Pros Use When All Else Fails

Tony Lolli

Wilderness
Adventures
Press, Inc.™

Belgrade, Montana

This book was made with an easy-opening, lay-flat binding.

© 2004 Tony Lolli


Cover, photos, and book design, © 2004 Wilderness Adventures Press, Inc.™

Published by Wilderness Adventures Press, Inc.™
45 Buckskin Road
Belgrade, MT 59714
800-925-3339
Website: www.wildadv.com
email: books@wildadvpress.com

First Edition

Printed in Singapore

Library of Congress Cataloging-in-Publication Data

Lolli, Tony.
  Go-to flies : 101 flies designed by professional guides for when all else fails / Tony Lolli.
    p. cm.
  Includes index.
  ISBN 1-932098-19-4
  1. Flies, Artificial. 2. Fly tying. I. Title.
  SH451.L65 2004
  688.7'9124--dc22
                                        2004024096


ISBN 1-932098-19-4

# Table of Contents

# Introduction

When the fishing is good, anyone with decent skills and knowledge can be a guide. But, as we all know, times can turn tough in a hurry. It's one thing if you're fishing on your own. It's quite another if you're on the professional end of a guide-client relationship. Then you have to get the sport hooked up—and I mean right now. Guides who want to stay in business always have a little magic tucked away for these difficult times.

Get any guide drunk enough and he'll admit that he has his little secrets, be it a technique, hidden fishing hole, or special fly. In this book, we'll focus on the last category: go-to flies that can be counted on to save the day. These flies result in a nice gratuity for the guides rather than an icy stare at the end of the day.

Of course, trying to pry information about these flies from guides around the country isn't always an easy task. It typically takes years of on-the-water experience and experimentation to arrive at such deadly patterns. The 101 flies presented here were shared by guides who were either inebriated when I contacted them (just kidding...maybe) or were simply willing to share the wealth for their own reasons. Either way, this book represents a rare chance to peek into the fly boxes of professional fly-fishing guides and learn some of their hard-earned secrets.

Many of these flies are simple and easy to tie because guides would rather spend time on the water than time sitting at their vises. This is especially true when guides have to provide flies for clients who have a knack for sacrificing them to rocks, trees, and passing vehicles.

Many go-to flies are purely the inventions of active imaginations—one might go so far as to say "overactive imaginations"—but you can't argue with their success. That's what this fly collection is all about: If they're good enough for fly-fishing guides who spend nearly every day of the season on the water helping paying clients catch fish, they'll work for you, too.

Some go-to flies came about by building on the effective characteristics of two or more existing flies. Others were the result of the guide's experience, observations, and knowledge about what makes a successful fly. A few were developed through plain old curiosity, while still others used innovative tying techniques to take advantage of new materials. And no doubt a fly or two was developed during late-night drinking sessions, never actually getting wet until the chips were down and every other fly had failed.

There's one thing you won't find here, and that is flies meant for hanging on the wall rather than for fishing. These guide patterns are sometimes downright ugly, often simple, and always effective enough to have found their way into the fly boxes of professional guides from across the U.S. and around the world. Hopefully, their proven success will encourage you to develop your own patterns based on what you learn here.

Some of the guides who created these flies are bona fide fly-fishing gurus with nationally recognized names. Others are lesser known. But they all have one thing in common: They get paid to take people fly fishing. And if they want repeat business, they'd better have some secret go-to flies standing by.

So here's your chance to impress your friends with how much you know about some seriously effective patterns that aren't advertised in every angling catalog. Best of all, you don't have to tell them you learned it from this book. You can begin your lecture by saying, "That reminds me of the time I was talking to a guide from Ireland…" Your secret is safe with me.

# TROUT

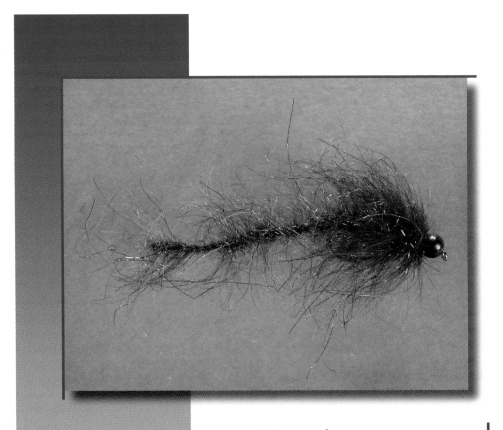

**1**

STALCUP'S
EXTENDED LEECH
*Tied by Shane Stalcup*

MATERIALS
Hook: Daiichi 1710, sizes 6–10
Thread: Olive, 6/0
Tail/Body: Sparkle leech dubbing,
    dirty olive
Weight: Black bead

Shane Stalcup (www.stalcupflies.com) has been making a living as a commercial tier and a materials-product designer for 20 years. He ties as many as 3,000 dozen flies per year and has produced 14 videos and two books, *Mayflies: Top to Bottom* and *Caddis Flies: Top to Bottom*. Somehow he also manages to find time to guide fly-fishing clients and write for a variety of national magazines.

Shane credits well-known tier John Betts with teaching him the technique employed here. When this method is used for a leech pattern, along with a bead head, the fly has a tremendous amount of movement. Even in between retrieves, the long fibers give the appearance of being alive. The leech dubbing comes in a full array of colors, so the possibilities are endless.

This fly was originally tied for trout, but it has caught its share of largemouth and smallmouth bass, too. And I bet a 10-inch version would be good for striped bass. How about a 24-inch fly for sharks? Or a 36-inch fly for black marlin?

Shane recalls a trip with his friend Bob David, an angler he claims could catch fish in a drainpipe. Bob was ahead on the fish count when Shane tried the Extended Leech for the very first time. Almost immediately, one trout after another fell to the fly. At the end of the day, Bob just had to know what Shane's secret was. Lucky for him—and the rest of us—Shane was happy to share his success. Now it's the only leech Bob uses.

## Tying Steps

1. Slide a bead onto the hook.

2. Tie in securely at the bend of the hook. This tie-in point will have to take a lot of pressure in the next step.

3. Make a loop with the thread and place a sparse amount of dubbing in it. Twist it tight. While maintaining the pressure, fold the dubbed loop over itself, relax the tension, and tie it down. If done right, the extension should twist into a rope, creating an extended body.

4. Form another dubbing loop and wrap a body up to the bead.

5. Scuff out the tail and body to make it fluffier.

**2**

PARACHUTE BWO
EMERGER
*Tied by Brad Befus*

MATERIALS
Hook: TMC 2457, sizes 14–24
Thread: Olive, 6/0
Tail/Shuck: Brown Antron or Z-lon
Abdomen: Olive/brown Antron dubbing
Wing Post: White closed-cell foam
Thorax: Muskrat fur
Hackle: Medium dun rooster

In 1988 fly-fishing guide and tier Brad Befus (blbefus@peoplepc.com) of Montrose, Colorado, began thinking about the perfect pattern for fish keying into the stage of the Blue-Winged Olive hatch when the emerging insect is struggling to free itself from the nymphal husk while stuck in the surface film. First, the fly had to remain suspended in the surface film as it floated along. Second, it had to be highly visible to the flyfisher, despite the small sizes often necessary for many tailwater fisheries. Third, it had to be buoyant enough for fishing choppy water, yet sparse enough to work well on spring creeks. Finally, it had to look like a good imitation of the nymphal shuck with the head poking out.

After experimenting with different materials, Brad eventually developed the Parachute BWO Emerger. The parachute provides the necessary flotation, yet maintains a low profile in the water. Using closed-cell foam for the post works particularly well because when trimmed it leaves a mushroom-shaped bulge above the hackle that keeps it from slipping off the post. The end of the white foam can be colored to increase its visibility.

The TMC 2457 hook provides enough weight to get the back of the fly into the surface film, leaving it in the same position as the natural. The Antron shuck and translucent abdomen offer a perfect representation of a nymphal shuck being left behind by an emerging dun. Finally, the dubbed muskrat imitates the head of the fly.

It's obvious that Brad put a lot of thought into this great little pattern. It quickly became his "confidence" fly for the *Baetis* hatch, and it probably will be yours, too, once you try it. Brad recently coauthored a book with John Berryman entitled *Basic Techniques for Successful Fly Tying*.

## TYING STEPS

1. Tie in a 2mm square strip of closed-cell foam approximately two hook-eye lengths behind the eye. Allow an inch to extend over the eye. This will later become the post.

2. Wrap over the foam toward the midpoint of the hook.

3. Stretch the foam and clip the excess at the midpoint.

4. Lift the remaining foam to a vertical position and wrap the base to make it stand up for the parachute wing post.

5. Lay down a thread base to a point approximately one-third of the way down the hook bend.

6. Tie in a sparse Z-lon trailing shuck that is equal in length to the hook shank.

7. Dub and wind a thin abdomen from the shuck's tie-in point to directly behind the wing post.

8. Tie in a hackle on the front side of the foam post. This should be secured on top of the hook, right at the base of the post.

9. Dub and wrap a thorax that is thicker at the post end and thinner toward the eye.

10. Take four or five wraps of hackle around the post and tie off behind the post. Clip the excess and whip finish at this location.

11. Clip the post so it is two eye lengths above the hackle wraps.

## Materials
Hook: Tiemco 2487, sizes 10–18
Thread: Black, 8/0
Hackle: Hungarian partridge
Head: Peacock herl
Thorax: Medium glass bead, sulphur/pearl
Body: Orange, medium Ultra Hot Wire

## 3

Trout
Hors d'Oeuvre
*Tied by Dave McCoy*

East or West, the same problem arises: What to try when the fish just aren't cooperating. This fly is Dave McCoy's answer. Dave runs Emerald Water Anglers (www.emeraldwateranglers.com) in Seattle, Washington, and he notes that this is a "does it all" pattern.

He reports that the Trout Hors d'Oeuvre is the product of guiding in areas where caddis are king for the majority of the fishing season: Colorado, Idaho, eastern Oregon, and eastern Washington. It is basically a blend of the best attributes of several different flies that already exist. This approach is quite often a successful one, and I'm surprised more tiers don't try it when inventing new patterns.

The fly works well on trout in nearly every set of conditions a river can throw at you. That's quite a claim, but since Dave's clients keep returning, he must be on to something important. In deep, slow-moving water he fishes it dead drift and deep or as a dropper behind a larger stonefly nymph. He gives it a steady to erratic stripping movement as the fly swings through the prime holding spots in the pool.

It also works well behind a hopper or Salmonfly pattern fished up against the banks during the summer.

## Tying Steps

1. Slide a glass bead onto the hook.

2. Wrap a thread base that ends halfway down the bend of the hook.

3. Tie in the wire halfway down the bend of the hook and wrap a body to the midpoint of the shank.

4. Whip finish, cut off the thread, and cement the end of the wire wraps.

5. Position the bead down against the wire.

6. Tie in ahead of the glass bead.

7. Tie on four or five strands of peacock herl.

8. Twist the herl with hackle pliers.

9. Wrap a herl collar the same diameter as the glass bead.

10. Tie on a single partridge hackle ahead of the herl and take two turns. The partridge fibers should extend just beyond the bend of the hook.

11. Whip finish and cement.

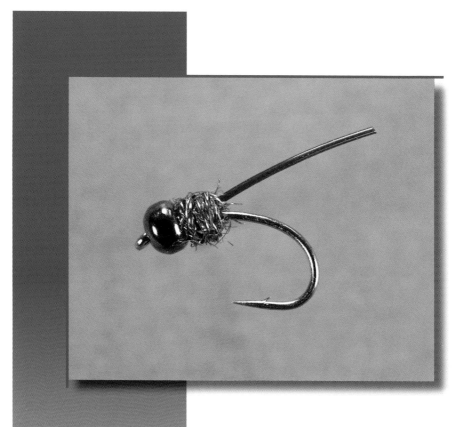

4

Red Bird
*Tied by Stan Benton*

## Materials
Hook: TMC 2487, size 18
Thread: Black, 8/0
Bead: Black, 2mm
Body: Red micro-tubing
Collar: Peacock Ice Dub

S tan Benton, the creator of this pattern, is manager and guide at Angler's Covey (www.anglerscovey.com) in Colorado Springs, Colorado. This fly ties up as quickly as you can pronounce its name. It only incorporates a couple of materials—and don't we all like simplicity whenever possible? Less time at the bench means more time on the water. As an added bonus, you won't feel like crying each time a fish, rock, or tree eats one.

Stan began experimenting with micro-tubing and was reminded of a pattern called the Rubber Duckie that was in use in the early 1990s. It had a piece of Spanflex tied on top of the hook and a dubbed collar. He decided to adapt that pattern by substituting flashier micro-tubing and adding a bead. Naming a pattern so that other anglers will remember it can be difficult, so Stan decided on an acronym: Red for the color and Beadhead Improved Rubber Duckie (Bird).

Stan's first testing was done on the Spinney Ranch section of the famous South Platte River. It was one of those days when the fish were down and not much feeding was taking place. He tried a number of flies that normally produce, but nothing seemed to work. Stan eventually ended up below a riffle at a hole about 4 feet deep. He could see a couple of fish working deep but just couldn't get them to take anything. In desperation, he finally decided to try the Red Bird. He quickly caught and released both fish. After that, Stan caught and released every fish he spotted. The Red Bird has had a secure spot in his fly box ever since.

## Tying Steps

1. Slide a bead onto the hook.

2. Lay down a short thread base and secure the bead against the eye.

3. Tie in a length of red micro-tubing behind the eye. Take a few turns of thread under the tubing so it sticks up at a 45-degree angle. It should be one and a half times the length of the shank.

4. Make a small collar of peacock-colored Ice Dubbing. The collar should be the same diameter as the bead.

Materials
Hook: Tiemco 106 TC, size 14–18
Thread: White, 8/0 Uni-Thread or UTC 70
Feelers: White Flouro-Fibre
Body: White thread
Dubbing: White STS Trilobal Dubbing
Eyes: Black small vinyl rib

5

Kolanda's
BTS Mysis # 1
*Tied by Rob Kolanda*

This has to be one of the strangest but most effective specialty flies I've ever seen, primarily due to the materials and techniques used.

Rob Kolanda from Rocky Mountain Anglers (www.rockymtanglers.com) in Boulder, Colorado, dreamed up this pattern. When I first saw the Mysis #1 I thought it was just an errant piece of flotsam that had fallen into the box along with some other flies he sent. It wasn't until I checked his written materials that I realized it was there by intent. It's a good thing, too. Just wait until you read about the success of his creation.

Rob developed this pattern while guiding on the Fryingpan River, which is known for its large Mysis-fed trout. Although many patterns had been developed to match the white, dead Mysis shrimp flushed into the river, there was no imitation for the live shrimp that slip through the turbines at Reudi Reservoir. The live shrimp are almost entirely clear, with a white tint. Earlier patterns typically incorporated epoxy, but it soon yellowed and lost the color of the naturals. So Rob experimented with Softex built over Flouro-Fibre. The soft, translucent material proved deadly on fussy fish.

As for the unusual name of this fly, it seems that one of Rob's clients was having the best day of his life. After landing a 12-pound fish the client gushed, "This is better than sex!" Thus was born the BTS pattern series, one of which is the Mysis #1.

Rob recently told me this pattern has also been successful on the tailwaters of the Blue and Taylor Rivers in Colorado, where Mysis shrimp are an important food source. It was responsible for a near-state-record fish of 23 pounds in January of last year. How's that for what's essentially an extruded fly?

## TYING STEPS

1. Lay down a thread base, which will also serve as the body of the fly.

2. Tie in feelers of Flouro-Fibre at the front of the fly. The front is actually at the bend of the hook.

3. Leave a couple of 6-inch pieces sticking out over the eye to be treated and trimmed later. These will form the extended body/tail.

4. Trim the feeler ends so that they stick out one shank length beyond the bend of the hook.

5. Tie in a piece of vinyl rib on top of the shank using figure-eight wraps. Trim close. This will leave small black spots as eyes.

6. Dub STS Dubbing around and behind the eyes.

7. Brush the dubbing down toward the hook point.

8. Apply Softex to the top of the body and tail. The long Flouro-Fibres and the STS dubbing will form the body. Some of the fibers will be combined with the dubbing and will be brushed down and trimmed even with the hook point. Be sure to trim any fibers on the top or side of body prior to applying the Softex, as any bumps or stray fibers will show.

9. Trim extra Flouro-Fibre behind the tail so it sticks out from the Softex about ⅛ inch.

**Materials**
Hook: TMC 2457, sizes 8–14
Thread: Black, 6/0
Bead: Silver for the black version, gold for the
  tan
Weight: Lead wire
Rib: Red copper wire
Tail: Goose biots
Body: Black Frog Hair or golden stone rabbit
Wing Case: Black goose biot for the black,
  natural turkey slips for the tan
Legs: Natural goose biots

**6**

North Fork
Special
*Tied by Tim Wade*

The North Fork Special is the invention of Tim Wade, owner of North Fork Anglers (www.northforkanglers.com) in Cody, Wyoming. It has proven so effective that there are now two versions—black and tan—to cover almost every need. Who could ask for more?

Tim designed the North Fork Special in the early 1990s as a general-purpose nymph. He needed something for fussy cutthroat trout in Yellowstone Park (that's right, not all cutthroats are gullible). The design evolved into a swimming nymph due to the angle and method of setting the goose biots. This fly actually rocks back and forth as it sinks, giving it that little something extra that trout find attractive. It can be fished on a dead drift or down and across the current during heavy caddis emergences or as a searching pattern.

Trout aren't the only species the North Fork Special has accounted for. Steelheaders in the Great Lakes tributaries in Michigan, Pennsylvania, Wisconsin, and New York swear by a black version in size 6 or 8. And bass and panfish in farm ponds across the country have fallen for a black North Fork Special fished around weed beds with a slow stripping action.

I'd say that's special enough, but I can't help but wonder how long until the South Fork Special turns up. If it does, I'm betting that Tim will be responsible for it.

## TYING STEPS

1. Pinch down the barb and slide on a bead.

2. Take 10 to 15 turns of lead wire and push the end up into the bead.

3. Secure the lead with thread and lay down a thread base that ends well down the bend.

4. Make a small ball of dubbing to flare the tails.

5. Tie in the tails so they flare away from each other (curving outward).

6. Tie in a length of copper wire.

7. Dub a thickly tapered body halfway up the hook shank.

8. Rib the body with several turns of copper wire.

9. Tie in goose biots for the wing case, with the curvature facing down against the hook. Tie them in one at a time, being sure to dub body material between the wing cases to create a thick thorax.

10. Trim the wing case biots so they give the appearance of multiple segments.

11. Tie in one goose biot on each side for legs, with the curvature facing outward. The biot tips should extend two-thirds the shank length and should point downward.

12. Dub a head with more body material, finishing up against the bead.

**7**

Collier's SnoBall
Chernobyl Beetle
*Tied by Dennis Collier*

### Materials

Hook: TMC 3679, sizes 10–16
Thread: Orange monocord
Body: Black foam (1mm) laminated to
orange foam (2mm)
Legs: Black small round rubber, two
pairs on each side
Indicator: Deer belly hair tied butts first
Glue: Zap-A-Gap

**D**ennis Collier is the head guide, casting instructor, and tier for Rocky Mountain Anglers (www.rockymtnanglers.com) in Boulder, Colorado. Like many western anglers, he has long fished with Chernobyl Ants, especially in Rocky Mountain National Park. He used them in smaller sizes, though, because ants are among the first insects to make their presence known after the long winter's sleep at 8,000 feet up in the Rockies. That's why the fish attack them with relish. I guess he figured that what works for ants should work just as well for beetles. The result was an effective, indestructible fly.

The big "snowball" indicator is made from white or fluorescent yellow deer hair and shows up easily, even for folks new to fly fishing. Orange, chartreuse, or hot pink also work well for the indicator.

So how good is this fly? Dennis has encountered flyfishers on-stream who, after swearing him to secrecy, show him one of his own patterns. Rocky Mountain Anglers can scarcely keep them in stock. A friend of Dennis's even fishes this pattern on the San Juan River in New Mexico, a river noted for technical hatches of miniscule insects. His friend reports that people often gather to watch him catch fish after fish with this "secret" fly.

The SnoBall Chernobyl Beetle is also a great stillwater fly, especially when strong winds are blowing the bugs into the water from surrounding vegetation. It even works well as an indicator fly when fished with something small like an RS2 or similar pattern.

## Tying Steps

1. Lay down a thread base from the eye to the bend and then back to a point one-third the shank length from the eye.

2. At this point, tie in the foam body with the black side up. Use only medium tension on the thread to avoid cutting through the foam. Then take two additional wraps with normal pressure to firmly attach it to the shank.

3. Loop two legs around the thread and pull them into the foam on the far side.

4. Loop two more legs and do the same thing on the near side.

5. Lift the front of the foam and take a few wraps, advancing the thread a short distance.

6. Pinch the foam down and take two wraps, creating segmentation.

7. Take a small bunch of deer hair and tie it in at the front segmentation.

8. Clip the deer hair to ⅛ inch. Whip finish at this spot.

9. Add a small bead of Zap-A-Gap along the thread from the bend to just behind the eye. This step is a must or the foam will rotate on the hook shank.

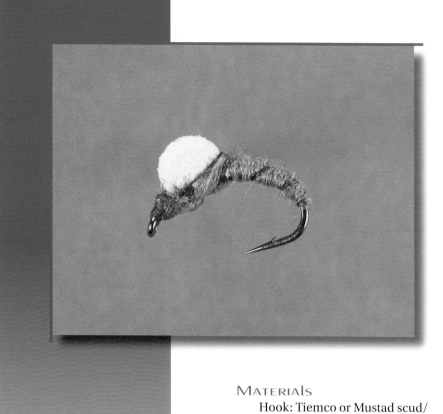

## Materials

Hook: Tiemco or Mustad scud/
shrimp/caddis, sizes 14–20
Thread: Red, 6/0
Bubble: White closed-cell foam
Body: Universal Vise, Blue-Winged
Olive

**8**

Jailbird
*Tied by Marla Blair*

uides can sometimes be secretive about what they're using, and that's actually how this fly got its name. The original pattern was called the Blair's Emerger. Guide Marla Blair (www.marlablair.com) and a friend were fishing in famous Cheesman Canyon on the South Platte River near Deckers, Colorado, when they invented this fly using fur from an old mink stole combined with white foam for a head. They hammered the fish.

Marla guides on the Farmington, Deerfield, Swift, and Westfield Rivers in Massachusetts and on the Farmington River in Connecticut. When she got home, she developed a variation using Blue-Winged Olive dubbing and a red rib. She was trying it out one day on the Swift River in Belchertown, Massachusetts, before the new version had even been named. She started getting hits on it right away and wanted to let her partner know what she was using. She thought the red rib looked like the stripes on convict uniforms she'd seen in old movies, so she yelled out that she was using a Jailbird. The name stuck.

Marla fishes this fly deep using a split shot and an indicator. She prefers a dead drift and says it works best in broken or fast water. Apparently, it imitates an emerging caddis or mayfly nymph. The weight gets it down to feeding depth, while the closed-cell foam holds it a bit above the split shot in the water column.

Based on some of the patterns and methods described by other guides, I'd guess this fly would also work well in the surface film as an emerger. The fact that it has a white bubble would make it a bit easier to follow, even though the bulk of the fly would ride below the surface.

## Tying Steps

1. Tie in white closed-cell foam at the midpoint of the hook shank.

2. Form the emerger bubble by folding the foam forward toward the eye. Tie down and then bring the foam back to the middle and tie off.

3. Bring the thread forward to the eye.

4. Dub on body material, keeping it thin.

5. Make figure-eight wraps around the foam, staying below it. Then wrap a thin body well down the hook bend.

6. Advance the thread—without dubbing—back up to the eye to create the rib.

7. Make a head, whip finish, and cement.

**MATERIALS**

Hook: Mustad 37160 or Varivas 999, sizes
14–18
Thread: Black, 8/0
Body: Green Haretron
Rib: Chartreuse Krystal Flash
Wing: Gray or olive Antron yarn combed out
(not spooled Antron)
Head: Arizona synthetic peacock dubbing
Legs: Dark speckled hen or dark partridge

9

K. T. FLASH PUPA
*Tied by Ken Tutalo*

Ken Tutalo's Baxter House B&B (www.baxterhouse.net) in Roscoe, New York, is so near the junction of the Beaverkill and Willowemoc Rivers that to get any closer you'd have to get wet. His go-to fly was inspired by Gary LaFontaine's Deep Sparkle Pupa, but it's easier to tie. Ken and his guides use this fly on browns, rainbows, and brookies, especially when nothing is hatching. Having guided in Ken's area, I can tell you that although these rivers see a lot of pressure, you can almost have the water to yourself when there aren't any bugs coming off.

This fly is successful because the combination of materials resembles a vulnerable stage in the life cycle of natural insects. In addition, the method for attaching the wing and the length of the legs create an undulating movement, even when fished on a dead drift.

Ken's favorite rig is a throwback to earlier times. He likes to dead-drift a classic three-fly setup. The top fly is a Stimulator or other large dry fly. Next comes a size 12 beadhead nymph about 15 to 18 inches below the dry. Finally, the Flash Pupa point fly is another 8 to 10 inches below the beadhead nymph.

A three-fly rig can be particularly effective at times because it offers the fish a veritable smorgasbord. Once the preferred pattern is identified you can swap out the nonproductive flies and offer the trout the hot pattern at different depths.

## Tying Steps

1. Start the thread at the eye and tie in one strand of Krystal Flash.

2. Wind the Krystal Flash well down the bend. Secure but do not trim.

3. Dub a tapered body toward the eye, leaving only enough room to attach the wing and head. The front end of the body must be the widest part so it can provide a shoulder against which to tie the wing.

4. Wind the Krystal Flash as a rib and tie off.

5. Cut a strand of Antron yarn and comb it out to separate the individual fibers. The wing should be sparse.

6. Tie in the Antron wing so that it covers the top and both sides of the body, but not the bottom. It should extend roughly half the shank length beyond the bend.

7. Dub a small spiky head.

8. Tie in a bunch of speckled hen fibers, beard-style. They should reach the hook point.

9. Dub just enough to cover the thread holding the legs.

10. Whip finish and cement.

**MATERIALS**

Hook: Dai-Riki 135 scud hook, sizes 12–16

Thread: Dark brown monocord, 3/0

Bead: Smoke color 6/0 glass

Tail: Natural ringneck pheasant (the small marabou feather found under each body feather)

Body: Rear third of peacock herl; then bead; front third of dark gray or brown llama dubbing

Shell: A slip of scud back

## 10

## SMOKED SNAIL
*Tied by Joe Brenton*

Joe Brenton of Angler's All, Ltd. (www.theflyman.com) in Littleton, Colorado, created this pattern. He reports that snails are something he encounters everywhere he fishes in the West, especially at mid-level and lower elevations.

Snail shells along his home waters had a translucent quality that he wanted to duplicate. Previous snail patterns that incorporated vinyl backs were somewhat productive; however, the appearance of depth and accurate coloration of a scud back over a glass bead is much more effective. The marabou tail represents the snail's foot, and its movement creates the illusion of life. Joe started with a Gary Borger pattern, adding the upgrades to make it look more natural.

The first time Joe's wife fished this pattern was in a gravel pit east of Fort Collins, Colorado. She suspended a size 12 Smoked Snail 18 inches under a strike indicator. Within an hour, she had broken off two snails on sizeable largemouth bass and caught four huge crappie. The pattern is also a great trout fly when dead-drifted in rivers.

## Tying Steps

1. Slide a bead onto the hook and lay down a thread base to the bend.

2. Tie in the tail at the bend, making it as long as the hook shank.

3. Tie in the shellback. Be sure the part you tie down covers only the rear third of the shank. If you tie it in too far forward you won't be able to slide the bead back later.

4. Tie in peacock herl and wrap a body over the rear third of the shank. Tie off and cement.

5. Slide the bead rearward to the middle of the shank and tie off.

6. Dub a rough llama thorax and wrap it in front of the bead.

7. Pull the shell forward and tie in behind the hook eye.

8. Whip finish and comb out a few llama hairs for legs.

MATERIALS
Hook: Mustad 3399, size 6–14
Thread: Black, 6/0
Body: Any gray fur dubbing, wrapped thickly
Case: Palmered natural red rooster
Thorax: Yellow Glo-Bug Yarn or dubbing
Legs: Speckled hen or dark partridge
Head: Black ostrich herl

11

CRUNCHY CAddis
*Tied by Ian James*

I an James from London, Ontario, developed this pattern. (Check out his entertaining website at www.ianjames.on.ca.) He describes this as one of his "first out of the box" nymphs. It's a general representation of many house-building caddis, which make shelters of sand, sticks, and small pebbles.

Ian credits two sources as the origin of the Crunchy Caddis: Cave's Caddis Larva from *Bob Church's Guide to Trout Flies* and the Wonder Nymph from Mike Dawes's *Flytier's Manual*. Ian thought he'd combine the best characteristics of each fly, and the Crunchy Caddis was born.

He says it's important to get this fly down to the bottom. Natural caddis just sort of slowly creep along, so a hand-twist retrieve is usually more productive than a wet-fly swing. Ian has tried weighting this pattern, but found that a split shot works better.

When he's guiding a first-timer, he often goes with a Crunchy Caddis because the strikes are aggressive and unmistakable. A beginner can feel the take and get more hookups. And the more chewed up the fly gets, the better it works.

This versatile fly has taken trout, steelhead, smallmouth bass, and carp. Ian even sent along a picture of a 15-pound carp that took a Crunchy Caddis on New Year's Day when the temperature was -3 degrees Celsius (that's 27 degrees for us Americans).

## Tying Steps

1. Tie in the thread well down the bend of the hook so that you still have plenty of room at the eye.

2. Tie in the trimmed rooster hackle by the tip. A bunch of these hackles can be teased out and trimmed ahead of time to speed up tying time.

3. Dub a body forward over three-quarters of the hook shank, leaving extra space between the body and the eye. The kind of fur used is not important, although the fly pictured here includes gray rabbit trimmed directly from the hide.

4. Palmer the rooster hackle and cut off excess. (When palmered, the hackle gives the appearance of spikes sticking out of the body.) Trim to the width of the hook gape.

5. Dub a pinch of yellow Glo-Bug Yarn.

6. Tie in another hackle feather by the tip to make the legs, but take only two turns. Don't over-dress the hackle or you will kill the action of the fly. Tie down and trim excess.

7. Tie in the ostrich herl by the thick end. Make a few close turns and trim off.

8. Whip finish and cement.

## Materials

Hook: Standard or 1X-long dry fly
Thread: Brown, 6/0 or 8/0
Tail: None
Rib: Very fine brass wire
Abdomen: Sparse brown Superfine
dubbing palmered over with an
undersized grizzly hackle
Underwing: Narrow slip of gray Swiss
Straw
Overwing: Wood duck flank fibers
Thorax: Same as abdomen, but fuller
Hackle: Broad collar of grizzly and
undersized grizzly for palmering

## 12

### Don's Schizo Stone
*Tied by Don Hershfeld*

D on's Schizo Stone comes from Don Hershfeld of Oakland, Maryland. He runs Streams and Dreams Retreat (www.streams-and-dreams.net) on the Youghiogheny River, where he's also the head guide.

This is Don's most productive fly on his home waters. On the surface, it gives the appearance of sitting still, yet also appears to be fluttering. Like many effective patterns, this one is tied sparsely except for the palmered hackle, which is necessarily heavy to help the fly sit up higher on the surface. This is also what gives it that fluttering appearance. Don notes that the naturals are rather long and lean insects, so for a good imitation it's necessary to avoid overdressing the fly.

Don has two methods for fishing this fly, depending on what's going on at the time. If the fish are rising, he slightly twitches the fly just as it comes into the trout's window. If the naturals are ovipositing (laying eggs), he drops the fly just behind, and to one side, of an actively feeding trout, enticing it to chase the fly before it gets out of range.

## TYING STEPS

1. Lay down a thread base to the bend.

2. Tie in a length of fine brass wire for ribbing.

3. Tie in an undersized grizzly hackle for palmering.

4. Dub a body and wind it forward slightly more than halfway.

5. Wind the rib to the same point, tie down, and trim.

6. Palmer the grizzly to the same point, secure, and then trim the top to make room for wing materials.

7. Tie in the Swiss Straw underwing. Trim to reach beyond the bend and cut a V-notch in the tail end.

8. Tie in the overwing of wood duck flank, extending it as far as the Swiss Straw.

9. Tie in another grizzly hackle.

10. Dub and wind the abdomen.

11. Wrap the hackle over the thorax, Stimulator-style.

12. Tie off, trim, and cement the head.

**MATERIALS**
Hook: Tiemco 200r, sizes 18–24
Thread: Brown, 8/0
Tail: Black pheasant tail fibers, split
Rib: Silver wire
Abdomen: Black marabou
Wing Case: Pearl Krystal Flash over Hareline
     Black Flash, covered by 5-minute epoxy
Thorax: Black possum
Legs: Hungarian partridge

13

BLACK DEATH
*Tied by Larry Watson*

Have you ever noticed how many fly pattern names refer to violence or other frightening things? There's the Purple Kinky Death, the Orange Mayhem, Thunder and Lightening, the Fallon Slayer, and many others. I wonder why there aren't more names like the Cuddly 'Cuda Catcher, the Tender Trout Taker, or the Fuzzy Fish Fooler?

Larry Watson of Denver, Colorado, sent this somber-sounding pattern along. He has guided for many years in the West and Alaska and says he combined the best features of several different flies to create this pattern.

Larry began with marabou, because of its ability to impart movement even in still water. He added silver wire not only for a little sparkle, but also to add durability to the marabou. The pearl Krystal Flash gives the wing case a shine like the natural's. And the Black Flash (under the Krystal Flash) looks like a darkening wing case that's getting ready to open. Larry notes that if the wing cases on naturals you're observing have turned black, it's a sign the bugs will be hatching within the hour.

This pattern imitates *Baetis,* and Larry fishes it all over the West. How good can a little fly like this be? Well, he reports catching a seven-pound rainbow at Grey's Reef on the North Platte River. I'll take that anytime.

## Tying Steps

1. Lay down a thread base.

2. Tie in two black pheasant tail fibers, one on each side of the hook. Be sure they splay out away from each other. They should be about as long as the hook shank.

3. Tie in a length of fine silver wire for ribbing.

4. Tie in four to six strands of black marabou and wrap forward about halfway to the eye.

5. Wrap the rib over the marabou in the opposite direction.

6. Tie in a strand of pearl Krystal Flash right up against the end of the abdomen.

7. Tie in some black Hareline Flash at the same spot.

8. Dub some black possum fur and wrap it to make a thorax that's fatter than the abdomen.

9. At the front of the abdomen, tie in some partridge fibers for legs. Make them stand out away from the body.

10. Pull the Black Flash over the thorax and secure it.

11. Do the same with the pearl Krystal Flash.

12. Make a small thread head, and then whip finish.

**MATERIALS**
Hook: Dry fly, sizes 12–14
Thread: Black, 6/0
Body: Black, gray-olive, or brown hare's ear
Wing: White poly

**14**

DUMMY FLY
*Tied by Roger Plourde*

I'm almost too embarrassed to tell you about this fly, but I know it works because I've watched Roger Plourde have a great deal of success with it. What I find most amusing is that this simple fly comes from a fly tier who literally spends days tying a single classic Atlantic salmon pattern. Go figure.

Roger hails from Plainville, Connecticut, and is known for his meticulously crafted salmon flies. You know the kind—128 different materials on a hook big enough to give a small man a hernia, and costing hundreds of dollars. I didn't know guys who tied those things also trout fished, but Roger does. He tells me he learned this fly from friends in Maine, where it's accounted for many landlocked salmon.

Although tying the pattern is simple, fishing it is even simpler. Roger uses an 8-foot leader with 4X tippet on a floating line. Sometimes he'll tie a second Dummy Fly to the bend of the first and fish them in tandem. He starts with a short cast directly across the current and then lets a belly form in the line so the fly cuts through the water as the current takes the line. After a few casts he'll move downstream and start the process again, covering all holding areas well. Most fish actually hook themselves on the tight-lined fly. It's a lot like riffle-hitching a Bomber fly for Atlantics.

The simplicity of the fly and the un-technical casting method make this pattern useful for introducing a new person to the sport of fly fishing. It never hurts to experience a little success before moving on to mastering the drag-free float.

## TYING STEPS

1. Dub a body from the bend three-quarters of the shank length toward the eye.

2. Tie in a white poly wing.

3. Continue dubbing to the eye.

4. Tie off and trim the wing to about ⅛ to ¼ inch.

MATERIALS
Hook: Tiemco 3202, sizes 12–16
Thread: Mono
Underbody: Mono
Body: Medium D-Rib, brown
Rib: Tan ostrich herl
Wing Case/Wing Buds: Brown Medallion
Sheeting
Thorax: Brown Hare's Ear Plus
Antennae: Mayfly tails, tan
Eyes: Burnt mono, marked black
Legs: Brown ostrich tips

## 15

### STALCUP'S FUZZY CADDIS PUPA
*Tied by Shane Stalcup*

Well-known commercial fly tier Shane Stalcup (www.stalcupflies.com) guides for Trout Trips (www.trouttrips.com) all over the state of Colorado. Like most guides, he believes that flies should be quick and simple to tie. While this fly doesn't fit that mold, it's more than worth the time it takes to tie it.

Shane has tried many pupa patterns over the years, but this is the one that fills his fly box these days. The ostrich rib makes the difference. When ostrich gets wet, it looks like tiny gills protruding around the body, just like those on natural caddis larvae. It's amazing that such a simple addition can make such a big difference, but it did.

He generally ties this pattern in tan, light olive, olive/brown, dirty yellow, and amber. It's a versatile pattern that works well in streams or lakes, and it's a great go-to fly.

## TYING STEPS

1. Make a thread base well down the bend.

2. Tie in a length of D-Rib so that when it's wrapped forward, the round side will be up.

3. Tie in ostrich for a rib.

4. Build an underbody of thread two-thirds up the shank.

5. Wrap the D-Rib forward, leaving a gap between wraps.

6. Wrap the ostrich forward, placing it in between the gaps in the D-Rib.

7. Trim the ostrich rib fibers as short as possible.

8. Tie in the wing case ahead of the underbody, and then advance the thread and tie in the mono eyes right up against the hook eye.

9. Tie in legs on each side.

10. Dub enough to make half the thorax.

11. Pull the wing case forward and tie it down at the midpoint of the thorax.

12. Add another pair of legs.

13. Dub the remaining length of the thorax.

14. Pull the wing case over the dubbing. You should be right behind the mono eyes.

15. Cut a narrow piece of wing case sheeting and figure-eight it on top of the eyes.

16. Pull one wingbud down and alongside the body and tie it into position. Repeat on the other side.

17. Trim the wingbuds so they reach no farther than the hook point.

19. Tie in two antennae with the tips out in front of the hook eye. Take the thread behind the eye, pull one antenna under the eye, and tie it down behind the eye. Repeat on the other side.

## MATERIALS

Hook: Nymph hook, sizes 16 or smaller
Thread: Black, 6/0
Body: Black Antron dubbing with gray
    guard hairs mixed in
Rib: Gold or copper wire
Tail: Gray goose biots
Wing Case: Turkey wing and one drop of
    epoxy

## 16

### THE MOOR
*Tied by Jim Dussias*

There's nothing complex about this fly, and that's the way Jim Dussias wanted it. Jim runs Oasis Angling (www.oasis-angling.com).

He usually fishes this fly in tandem with one or two other flies, sometimes running it below a dry fly that acts as a strike indicator. Often he'll fish two Moors below the dry: one unweighted and one tied with a bead head to keep it below the first. This way he has the entire water column covered.

He and two clients recently fished the Moor in the cold of December on an Iowa spring creek. (It's true; there really are spring creeks in Iowa.) The Moor out-fished every other nymph they tried. It accounted for over 20 large browns in four hours of fishing over fussy trout. Jim believes the trout assume it's a tiny stonefly nymph or snow midge pupa.

Who would have ever thought that epoxy might work as a wing case? I guess it always pays to experiment.

## Tying Steps

1. Tie in a piece of gold wire at the bend for ribbing.

2. Also at the bend, make a tail of split goose biots.

3. Dub a rope and include guard hairs for a buggy appearance.

4. Wind the body, building an abdomen two-thirds up the shank.

5. Tie in a slip of turkey wing.

6. Wind the wire forward to segment the abdomen, and then tie off.

7. Continue winding a wider thorax, stopping behind the eye.

8. Pull the turkey slip forward to make a wing case and tie off behind the eye.

9. Pick out the guard hairs with a bodkin to create the appearance of legs.

10. Make a wing case bulge by adding a large drop of epoxy to the top of the turkey wing case.

11. Whip finish and cement the threads.

## MATERIALS

Hook: TMC 200R, sizes 8–16
Thread: Olive, 6/0
Tail: Golden goose biots
Abdomen: Wapsi Fly's Ultra Wire,
  hot yellow and black
Wing Case: Medallion Sheeting
Thorax: Peacock herl
Legs: Golden goose biots
Head: Gold bead

## 17

### WIRED STONE NYMPH
*Tied by Brad Befus*

Brad Befus (blbefus@peoplepc.com) sent along this pattern. He's a guide and contract fly designer for Umpqua Feather Merchants, so his qualifications are certainly well established. His flies catch fish; it's that simple.

Medallion Sheeting is used to form the wing case segments over the top of the thorax on the Wired Stone Nymph. This is one of the most sturdy and user-friendly materials that Brad has ever found for wing cases and shellbacks. It has better durability properties than turkey or goose quill. Unlike those natural materials, Medallion Sheeting doesn't separate when handled during the tying process or in the water. As a bonus, this material is thin, pliable, and easy to work with.

So there you have it: an effective, bombproof stonefly nymph pattern.

## Tying Steps

1. Slide a bead up to the eye.

2. Lay a thread base down the bend to a point above the barb.

3. Dub a small ball for splaying the tails.

4. Tie a goose biot on each side of the dubbing ball, then advance the thread to the bead.

5. Place one color of Ultra Wire along the far side of the hook. Wrap the wire over itself, starting at the bead and wrapping back to the tail. Leave a long piece of wire pointing out past the tail.

6. Do the same thing with the second color of wire, but start it on the near side of the shank.

7. Tightly wrap the wire and shank with thread. Next, create a tapered underbody from the tail to the midpoint of the hook shank using thread wraps.

8. Start wrapping the colored wires around the underbody from the tail to the end of the underbody. Keep the wires parallel as you wrap them, which creates a two-colored, segmented body.

9. Tie in the wing case of Medallion Sheeting—the same width as the hook gape—at the midpoint, just ahead of where the body ends.

10. Tie in the first set of legs at this same point.

11. Tie in four strands of peacock herl and wrap forward one-third of the thorax length. Tie off, but don't trim. Leave the strands lying along the shank.

12. Pull the wing case forward and tie down. Wrap several turns of thread over the wing case toward the bead and then back to the tie-in point.

13. Fold the wing case back and tie down.

14. Tie in a pair of legs.

15. Wrap the same strands of peacock to start the second segment of the thorax.

16. Repeat steps 11 through 14 to complete the second segment.

17. Repeat steps 11 through 14 to complete the third thorax segment.

18. Clip the excess peacock and take several wraps of thread between the wing case and the bead. By creating the segments of the wing case and thorax in the manner described above, the peacock herl is quite secure under the Medallion Sheeting.

## Materials

Hook: TMC 5263, sizes 2–6
Thread: Rusty brown UTC
Eyes: Gold Dazle-Eyes
Body: Dubbing blend of 80-percent golden brown Ice Dub and 20-percent UV cinnamon Ice Dub
Rib: Fine gold Largartun wire
Wing: Two furnace brown Whiting hen neck hackles on each side of one bright yellow Whiting hen neck hackle
Collar: Three wraps of bright yellow plus three wraps of furnace brown Whiting hen neck
Head: Chocolate brown Ice Dub

## 18

Collier's PRS
Matuka
*Tied by Dennis Collier*

Sometimes even the most well-known fly can benefit from a makeover, becoming more effective as a result. Dennis Collier, a guide from Rocky Mountain Anglers (www.rockymtanglers.com) in Boulder, Colorado, knows this truth very well. He had used the Platte River Special (PRS) for many years, but he was also aware that due to its construction the PRS would often foul and lose its most valuable qualities. Here's how he improved on the design.

The Matuka-style wing solved the fouling problems of the original PRS. However, the improvements didn't end there. The next step was to incorporate the effective color scheme of the original. Dennis also added Dazle-Eyes to give it some extra appeal. The eyes add a bobbing motion to the fly, which can be enhanced by using an open loop knot and giving the fly a jerky retrieve.

Dennis recommends fishing this fly hard to the bank. Allow it to drift downcurrent for a short distance, and then lower the rod tip almost to the water and give it an erratic stripping action on the crosscurrent swing. This technique prevents fish from going undetected when they pick up the fly because there's little slack in the line. Finally, Dennis advises anglers to hang tight to the rod because the strikes are savage. I like that part.

## Tying Steps

1. Lay down a thread base.

2. Tie in eyes on the bottom of the hook shank, slightly back from the hook eye.

3. Tie in a piece of wire directly above the barb for ribbing.

4. Dub a body and wrap forward to just behind the hook eye. Take some figure-eight turns around the eyes on the way.

5. Make the wing hackles twice the length of the shank. Strip the bottom fibers off the hackles where the wing will touch the body. Tie them in behind the eye, and then wet your fingers and stroke the wing fibers up.

6. Wrap the ribbing forward through the fibers of the hackles to just behind the eyes.

7. Tie in two hen neck hackles behind the eyes, and take three turns of each color.

8. Make a head by dubbing a small amount of Ice Dub right behind the eyes. Figure-eight around the eyes and make a small head.

9. Use the "hook" side of a piece of Velcro to roughen up the body and head. This will soften the profile and release the UV fibers in the dubbing.

**19**

ARCTIC GRAYLING
BETTER GETTER
*Tied by Reed Morisky*

MATERIALS
Hook: Mustad 94840, size 12
Thread: Black, 8/0
Body: Rainy's Fly Foam, formed out with
    a leather punch
Legs: Dry-fly hackle
Indicator: Bright green foam (glued to
    the body before it's tied onto the hook)
Attractor Spot: Orvis Holofleck glue

I suppose the very first thing you have to do if you really wanted to catch an arctic grayling is travel to where they live. The second would be to take Reed Morisky's advice and tie one on—one of his flies, that it.

Reed runs Arctic Grayling Guide Service (www.wildernessfishing.com) out of Fairbanks, Alaska. He can fix you up with a guided fishing trip or an unguided overnight stay at a secluded streamside cabin. He can also provide you with a can of pepper spray as a deterrent for "curious" bears. How many other guides need to assure you of that?

Graying like a floating fly, and this one will float for hours. With the addition of the indicator color, this fly is easy to see even under low-light conditions at dawn and dusk. This is particularly important for a grayling fly because the fish's rise form is often very slight. A fly that sits lower on the surface might be taken with so little commotion that the strike goes unnoticed.

Although the foam floats well by itself, Reed treats it with silicone to make it float even better. Apparently, it's not possible for a grayling fly to float too high, which is good news for all you dry-fly fanatics out there.

## Tying Steps

1. Tie in a short thread base near the center of the shank.

2. Tie the foam body with the colored end toward the eye. Leave one-third of the body ahead of the tie-in point and two-thirds sticking out behind. The first wraps must not be tied in too tightly or the thread will cut the body in two. Gradually tighten the tension as you add thread wraps, while at the same time widening the space between the wraps. This method leaves a short thorax ahead of the tie-in point and an extended body behind.

3. Secure the body and thread wraps with cement.

4. Tie in a hackle for legs.

5. Tie off and cut thread.

6. Add one drop of Holofleck to the underside of the foam body where the fish can see it and another on top of the indicator to make it more visible to you.

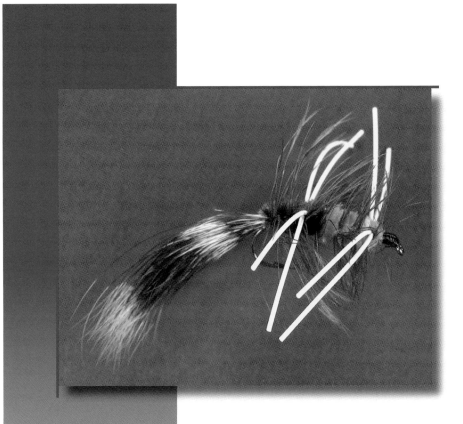

20

SUPER YUK BUG
*Tied by Dan Hurzeler*

MATERIAlS
Hook: Mustad 3399A, sizes 2–8
Thread: Black, 6/0
Tail: Red squirrel tail
Body: Green and orange chenille,
    palmered brown hackle
Legs: White rubber

an Hurzeler, who runs Fin Chasers (208-557-0333) in Idaho Falls, Idaho, tells me this fly began as his attempt to mate the Girdle Bug and the Super Renegade. Both of these "parent" flies worked great on the South Fork of the Snake River during stonefly hatches, and Dan wanted to incorporate the best characteristics of each.

Dan thinks the rubber legs account for the fly's success. Twitching the retrieve seems especially attractive to trout. He also fishes his invention as a wet fly, both with and without weight, using a stripping retrieve.

His first on-the-water experimentation with the Super Yuk Bug was during a hatch of the big bugs. He tested it by fishing a two-fly rig: the new one versus a traditional stonefly pattern. The crossbreed out-fished the established pattern and quickly became one of Dan's go-to flies.

The Super Yuk Bug has worked well on the Madison and Big Hole Rivers in Montana and the Henry's Fork and South Fork of the Snake River in Idaho. It will likely take fish anywhere big stoneflies are found, including larger rivers in New England. I'll be trying it this summer for landlocked salmon.

## Tying Steps

1. Tie in a long tail of red squirrel tail at the bend, extending an inch beyond the hook.

2. Also at the bend, tie in some green chenille and then a brown hackle.

3. About a quarter of the way toward the eye, tie in a double strand of white rubber legs. Use figure-eight wraps to make them stand out perpendicular to the hook shank.

4. Wrap the green chenille forward to the midpoint of the hook and tie off and trim.

5. Tie in a length of orange chenille.

6. Tie in another double set of rubber legs a quarter of the way behind the eye.

7. Wrap the orange chenille forward, making the forward set of rubber legs stick out as before.

8. Palmer the brown hackle to the eye.

9. Make a head, whip finish, and cement.

10. Split all four sets of the double strands of white rubber to make a total of eight legs.

**21**

Fox's Poopah
*Tied by Tim Fox*

MATERIALS
Hook: TMC 2302, size 14, or 3769, size 12
Thread: Tobacco brown Flymaster 6/0 or
    rusty brown Ultra 7/0
Body: Vernille, olive or poopah brown
Underbody: Medium pearl tinsel
Rib: Medium-fine gold wire
Legs: Partridge or hen back
Antennae: Wood duck
Head: Brown or black ostrich

Tim Fox, a guide with The Fly Shop (www.theflyshop.com) in Redding, California, developed this fly 10 years ago. Since then, various companies have ripped it off, but it's still Tim's baby. He reports that even though the term pupa is pronounced "pew-pa," so many people mispronounce it as "poo-pa" that it was a natural for the fly's name.

The body color can be matched to local caddis hatches, but in Tim's experience, tan and olive produce best. During the summer months, a tan Poopah in size 14 is *the* fly for the Lower Sacramento River.

Tim figures this fly works well because it looks like a real caddis pupa, whether it's rolling along the bottom or swinging just below the surface. The colors are imitative and the profile realistic.

You'd think this fly would only be good for trout, but customers have told Tim they've even used it to catch Atlantic salmon, and an olive version on a heavier hook works well on coastal steelhead in early spring.

## TYING STEPS

1. Lay down a thread base to a spot just above the hook point.

2. Tie in a piece of gold wire.

3. Tie in some pearl tinsel and wind forward to make the body.

4. At this point, tie in a length of Vernille that extends a short distance beyond the bend of the hook.

5. Singe the tail end of the Vernille to prevent it from fraying.

6. Wind the wire forward, ribbing the body and securing the Vernille to the hook. Tie the wire down.

7. Tie in two wood duck fibers, pointing rearward over the back and about the same length as the body.

8. Tie in partridge hackle beard-style with the points extending almost to the bend of the hook.

9. Tie in ostrich herl and wind a full collar, making a head.

10. Tie off, whip finish, and cement the thread head.

**MATERIALS**
Hook: Tiemco 200R, size 10
Thread: Mossy green, 6/0
Tail: Elk hair
Abdomen: Mossy green yarn
Body Hackle: Grizzly
Wing: Elk hair
Thorax: Mossy green yarn
Hackle: Grizzly

**22**

YAKIMA SKWALA
STONEfly
*Tied by Mark Pederson*

Ever had a fish bump a Stimulator but refuse to take it? Come on, 'fess up. It happens to all of us at times. Mark Pederson runs the Dry Fly Angling Company (www.dryflyangling.com) in Snoqualmie, Washington, and it happened to him, too. When the wild rainbows of Washington's upper Yakima River started refusing his client's gaudy patterns he had to come up with a quick solution, and this fly is how he did it. It worked for the clients, and it will work for you.

Mark thought that the traditional Stimulator patterns were too bushy to match the Skwala stonefly so he designed a scaled-down version. The predominant size of the upper Yakima Skwala is a size 8, but Mark went down to a size 10. He describes it as a barbered version of the original. The flush-floating profile presents a more realistic surface impression in slack water, and the mossy green underbelly seems to pull trout in.

The fly is most effective when the female Skwala return to the river to lay eggs; when spent adults fall on the surface and die; and on warm, gusty afternoons when the naturals get blown onto the water.

Although the Skwala lives in swift, well-oxygenated pocket water, adults can turn up anywhere the wind takes them. An especially good area is a section of thick, brushy bank over prime holding water. Here, the naturals will fly up into the trees, and either the wind or the mating urge will send them onto the river and into the trout's dining room.

## TYING STEPS

1. Starting one-third the shank length back from the eye, lay down a thread base to the bend.

2. Cut and stack a small amount of elk hair for the tail that's equal to half the hook gape. Bind the hair tightly so it flares out. This is really a representation of an egg sack, not a traditional tail.

3. Tie in a grizzly hackle for palmering.

4. Tie in yarn and wrap an abdomen to the point where the thread base began. Tie off.

5. Palmer the hackle forward to this same spot and tie off.

6. Clip the top of the hackle so the wing lies flat.

7. Cut and stack elk hair to tie in as a wing. Make the wing lie flat by walking the thread back a short distance and then winding it forward to the tie-in point.

8. Tie in a hackle and yarn for the thorax.

9. Wrap the yarn to the eye, tie off, and trim.

10. Palmer the hackle with three turns. Tie off and trim.

11. Whip finish a head, trim, and cement.

12. Trim the underside of the palmered hackle fibers flush with the body.

**23**

SPRUCE-A-bOU
*Tied by Tom Loe*

MATERIAlS

Hook: Tiemco 3769 or 5262, 2X heavy and 2X long, size 4–8
Thread: Black, 6/0, and red, 8/0, unwaxed
Body: Red premium or small or medium Ultra Chenille
Rib: Small gold oval tinsel
Underwings: Golden olive or ginger marabou
Sides: Golden badger hackle
Overwing: Peacock herl and pearl Krystal Flash
Head: Grizzly hackle
Gill Band: Red thread

Need an imitation for a squawfish? Tom Loe did. He runs Sierra Drifters Guide Service (www.sierradrifters.com) out of Mammoth Lakes, California, and he needed a new fly for fishing the eastern Sierra waters where he guides. This is what he developed.

Tom's streamer looks like a sculpin or a squawfish, both of which are found in big numbers in the eastern Sierras. Since big fish eat little fish, this fly is a favorite of the large browns on his home waters.

Fishing this fly effectively requires a moderate to heavy sink-tip or full-sinking line. The Spruce-a-bou should be fished slowly along the bottom, with erratic movements made by pulling the line or twitching the tip of your rod quickly and aggressively, although not so much that you leave a lot of slack in the line. Too much, and you'll miss the take.

Tom recommends casting this fly quartering downstream to the far bank. Just after the cast, throw in an upstream mend to add enough slack line for the fly to sink quickly. Once the fly reaches the strike zone, pull it upstream with 4- to 6-inch tugs. Let the fly pause occasionally—and don't forget to hang on when you get a savage strike.

## TYING STEPS

1. Lay down a thread base to the bend of the hook.

2. Tie in a piece of chenille and oval tinsel ribbing at the bend.

3. Wrap the chenille forward about half the distance to the eye, tie off, and trim.

4. Wrap the rib forward, tie off, and trim.

5. Turn the hook over and tie in the marabou underwing beneath the hook shank.

6. Turn the hook right side up and tie in another marabou underwing above the shank. Both underwings should extend just past the hook bend.

7. Top off with peacock herl followed by four to seven pieces of Krystal Flash.

8. Prepare matching badger feathers by stripping off the fluff but leaving the broad part near the butt ends.

9. Tie in the badger on each side, forward of the body. The hackle tips should cross at the rear of the fly and the ends should extend one-third the length of the shank past the bend.

10. Tie in a grizzly hackle ahead of the body and take four to six wraps. Trim it flat at top and bottom.

11. Make an elongated thread head.

12. Tie a gill band of red thread at the head.

13. Cement head wraps.

**Materials**
Hook: Scud hook, size 14
Thread: Black, 8/0
Body: Red squirrel tail
Collar: Red Banty chicken hackle

24

Vermont Special
*Tied by George Clifford*

B eing from Vermont myself, when I saw this fly's name I somehow thought maple syrup might play a prominent role in its construction. However, George Clifford from Montpelier, Vermont, had something else in mind, although it does involve a connection to food.

George owns the Brookies Guide Service (www.vermontbrookies.com), and he explains that this fly took shape one night over dinner. He happened to be dining on venison stew "made entirely from locally produced ingredients." He had been reading books by Flick and Schwiebert and noticed their flies had been mostly created from locally procured natural materials. Of course, those fly-tying pioneers were working in the days before synthetics became popular.

Anyway, at this point he jumped up on his chair and shouted, "Have we lost the ingenuity of the early fly tiers? Have we become complacent with what's available on the shelves of our local fly shops? I need an organic fly made from local materials!" His wife told him that if he knew what was good for him, he'd get down off the furniture. But it was too late. His mind was made up—and the Vermont Special was born.

George fishes this fly as an emerger floating in the film or rising from the bottom, wet fly–style. He also uses it as a dropper below a dry fly. The natural color imitates the color of many nymphs in the Northeast. It's proven successful during the Sulfur hatch, as well as caddis hatches.

In this case, the important natural materials are red squirrel tail and Red Banty chicken hackle. If you live in the northern portion of the United States or in Canada, finding the former in the woods should be no problem (although harvesting them with a small-caliber rifle is another matter). Banties are easier to find, but you may have a hard time persuading an unbelieving farmer that you just want his bird for the feathers.

## Tying Steps

1. Wrap a thread base to the bend of the hook.

2. Make a dubbing loop and dub squirrel hair using as much red as possible.

3. Wrap a body, stopping two eye lengths behind the hook eye.

4. Tie off and trim the body to size.

5. Tie in a hackle by the butt end and wrap three or fours turns, wet fly–style.

6. Make a head, whip finish, and cement.

**Materials**
Hook: Kamisan B40, sizes 12–20
Thread: Black, 8/0
Weight: Lead or copper wire or
tungsten bead
Body: Audio cassette ribbon
Collar: Peacock herl

25

CCR Caddis
*Tied by Chris Dore*

Chris Dore runs Trout Safaris, Ltd. (www.troutsafaris.co.nz) in Queenstown, New Zealand. It seems he was driving along—no doubt on his way to go fishing—when his cassette player began chewing up yet another tape. As he contemplated giving it a toss out the window, Chris noticed the color was a good match for the body of the horned cased caddis. He managed to save a few feet of the tape and tucked it away for use later. Back home at the tying vise, he came up with the CCR Caddis. Why that name? Creedence Clearwater Revival, of course.

Chris says the large trout of New Zealand, in general, and of the famous Mataura River, in particular, are becoming wary of the standard popular patterns. These wild native fish need only a couple of bad experiences to become well educated. As a result, Chris has been switching to well-presented newer patterns to get the job done for his clients.

Caddis are weak swimmers that drift naturally near the streambed. This suggests the need for a weighted nymph that can be dead-drifted down in the strike zone. And that's just the way Chris recommends fishing the CCR Caddis. Incorporating too much weight into the body creates a profile that's too fat to match the naturals, so if a few wraps of lead or copper wire aren't enough to get the proper sink rate, just add a tungsten bead.

Chris's favorite searching combination is a pair of these flies, which often find success even when nothing is hatching on the Mataura. It also produces on the high-country rivers of Central Otago and in the meandering lowland rivers of the southern plains. It's a fly that should work well anywhere caddis are present, particularly in areas where the fish see a lot of artificial flies every day.

## Tying Steps

1. Stretch out audio tape to create a thinner, easier-to-wrap ribbon. Pull until it's almost at the breaking point. The tape may contract a little, but most of the stretch will remain.

2. Lay down a thread base from the eye to a point halfway down the bend.

3. Tie in a length of tape at the bend.

4. Tie in a length of lead or copper wire (depending on how deep you want this fly to sink). Advance the thread, and then wrap the wire forward.

5. Keep the tape under tension as you wrap a smooth body over the wire. Tie off.

6. Tie in peacock herl and wrap a collar.

7. Whip finish and cement.

### MATERIALS
Hook: Tiemco 2487, sizes 12–16
Thread: Tan, 8/0
Shuck: Ginger Z-lon
Body: Small D-Rib
Thorax: Bleached ginger possum
Post: Rainy's foam post
Hackle: Grizzly by Whiting

## 26

### CALLIBAETIS
### PARACHUTE
### EMERGER
*Tied by Larry Watson*

L ongtime guide and fly-fishing-industry authority Larry Watson from Denver, Colorado, sent in this pattern, noting that it's his favorite *Callibaetis* imitation for lakes. He had tried other *Callibaetis* patterns that used biots for the abdomen, but he wanted a more translucent appearance. In addition, he needed a material that would let the abdomen sink into the film, not float it like the biots did. After some experimentation, he hit on using small D-Rib, which accomplished both the translucent look and the low-in-the-water position of an emerging natural trying to break free of the surface film.

Larry has used this pattern on many of Colorado's toughest lakes, including Spinney Mountain Reservoir and North Delaney Butte Lake. It has also been effective in spring creeks like Armstrong and Nelson Creeks in Montana. Larry reports that it has accounted for many trout in the 5-pound range. While there may be no honor among thieves, fly guides are required to accept each other's claims because you never know when you may need some other guide to nod his head in agreement when you start to explain to a client why he should have been here yesterday.

## TYING STEPS

1. Lay down a thread base halfway to the bend of the scud hook.

2. Tie in a foam parachute post just behind the eye.

3. Return the thread to a point halfway down the bend and tie in a shuck of several strands of ginger Z-lon. The shuck should be slightly shorter than the hook shank.

4. Tie in two small D-Ribs.

5. Advance the thread back to the foam parachute post.

6. Wrap the D-Ribs to create a segmented abdomen. Be careful to keep them parallel to each other; don't let them cross.

7. Dub some ginger possum and wrap a thorax slightly larger in diameter than the abdomen.

8. Tie in a grizzly hackle on the foam post and take two or three turns. Tie off the parachute.

9. Make a thread head, whip finish, and cement.

**MATERIALS**
Hook: Tiemco TMC 2488H, sizes 18–24
Body: Rusty dun thread, 8/0
Head: Black thread, 8/0
Wing and Tail: Lemon barred wood duck

## 27

CLINT'S EMERGER
*Tied by Clint Wilkinson*

Sometimes good things come in small packages—at least when it comes to picky trout in slow, clear water. Clint Wilkinson (www.whiteriver-flyfishing.com) from Gassville, Arkansas, invested lots of time in observing the habits of large trout on many Arkansas tailwater fisheries. What he saw caused him to realize the importance of midges as a primary food source, despite of the huge difference between the size of the trout and the size of the insect. His hard-earned knowledge led him to develop a simple and effective midge pattern that has served him well for several years.

In fast water, Clint recommends fishing the midge under a small strike indicator or dry fly, with a small split shot about 6 inches above the midge. A dead drift and quick hook-set are both important, or the trout will drop the fly and you'll be left wondering if that slight hesitation was a fish or a rock. When in doubt, set the hook and see what happens.

In slow water, this midge pattern can be fished without weight or as a single fly up in the surface film. When the option presents itself, Clint recommends fishing the midge in riffles rather than pools. In those areas, trout don't get much time to look this general imitation over before deciding to eat it.

But doesn't the old saw about "big flies for big trout" still hold true? Well, according to Clint, you shouldn't put too much stock in that saying when it comes to tailwater trout. He's used this midge to take trout up to 24 inches long on the White and Norfork Rivers in his home state.

## Tying Steps

1. Wrap a tight thread base to the bend of the hook.

2. Tie in two to four strands of wood duck breast fibers for a tail.

3. Wrap a tight thread base over the wood duck, back to where the first thread base started.

4. Wrap a third tight thread base back to the bend.

5. Wrap a final tight thread base up to the starting point. If done properly, the body will be smooth and provide a shoulder for the wing to set against.

6. Tie in four to six wood duck fibers as a wing. The wing should stand off the body at an angle and fan out slightly.

7. Whip finish and switch to black thread.

8. Build up a black head that is slightly thicker than the dun body.

**MATERIALS**
Hook: Mustad 9672 streamer, size 12
Thread: Olive, 6/0
Tail: Olive marabou
Body: Olive V-Rib
Wing Case: Dark turkey slip
Thorax: Red glass bead with olive Bug Fur
Eyes: Hourglass lead eyes

# 28

El Loco Diablo
*Tied by Barry Shrader*

This is not the start of a Spanish lesson. Instead, it's the name of a go-to fly created by Barry Shrader from Tishomingo, Oklahoma. Barry runs the Old West Fly Shop and Blue River Guide Service (www.getawayok.com/getawayok_100 .htm). His other fly-fishing creations are also named in the Old West tradition. They include the Lone Ranger, Belle Star, and Curly Bill.

Most flyfishers seeking rainbows on the Blue River in southern Oklahoma still rely on the Woolly Bugger. It's certainly an effective fly, but after many long days on the water Barry discovered another: the Olive Damselfly. However, he wanted a simpler version of the existing patterns to reduce his time at the vise and increase his time on the water.

The main difference between the standard damsel patterns and the Loco Diablo is the use of a glass bead to make the thorax. Barry tried several variations using red, green, and amber beads. After testing the variations, he found that the red bead out-fished the other two colors at a rate of 2-to-1.

The Loco Diablo can be fished using a variety of techniques. In a fast riffle, Barry likes the high-stick method, with only the leader in the water. He'll raise and lower the fly throughout the drift to simulate an emerging insect. It can also be fished like a streamer, by casting across and slightly downstream. If there's no take on the drift, he'll have his clients closely watch the swing. Fish will often take the fly as it rises to the surface at the end of the swing. Failing that, he recommends a smooth, rhythmic twitch during the drift.

## TYING STEPS

1. Place the hook in the vise upside down.

2. Wrap a short thread base.

3. Tie on hourglass eyes using figure-eight wraps, then tie off and cement the threads.

4. Slide a glass bead over the hook point and up to the eyes.

5. Turn the hook right side up.

6. Secure the glass bead up against the eyes with thread.

7. Lay down a thread base to the bend of the hook.

8. Tie in a tail of marabou that's equal to the length of the shank.

9. Tie in the V-Rib with the flat surface facing up.

10. Advance the thread to the bead.

11. Wrap the V-Rib to the glass bead and tie off. Cut excess.

12. Tie in turkey slip for the wing case.

13. Apply dubbing to thread.

14. Make two wraps behind the glass bead and two more in front.

15. Fold the wing case over the glass bead and dubbing. Tie down.

16. Advance the thread in front of the eyes and pull down the remaining turkey slip. Tie in and trim excess.

17. Pick out dubbing to make legs.

18. Make a thread head and cement.

MATERIALS
Hook: Gamakatsu C12, size 16
Thread: Color to match body, 8/0
Wing Post: White poly yarn
Hackle: Grizzly or brown
Body: Dubbed olive hare's ear

## 29

FIRST CHOICE
*Tied by David Murray-Orr*

Some old tiers claim there's really nothing new under the sun in the world of fly tying. Well, sit up and pay attention because this one is the exception.

We all know it's difficult to finish off a parachute pattern when you have to lift the hackle in order to get the head completed up near the eye—right? Now David Murray-Orr, who runs Southland Flies and Guides (www.mataura.co.nz) in New Zealand, provides an alternative that allows you to tie off at the wing post. He paid close attention while learning this technique from a master Japanese fly tier, and he incorporated it into the First Choice for several reasons.

First, this method is easier than the old way of dealing with parachutes. In addition, by wrapping the thread under the hackle, it can be lifted away from the body. This allows the body to sink farther in the surface film. Why is this important? Suppose the fish are focused in on emergers *before* they get to the surface film? You've seen those frustrating rise forms: The water bulges and fools you into thinking they're taking duns. With this tying method, you can get the fly to their feeding zone in the water column by increasing the distance from the body to the hackle. Thus, the fly rides lower. Pretty neat, huh?

When using waterproof dressing with this fly, apply it only to the wing post and hackle—not the body. To maximize effectiveness the body must soak up water and sink to the point where it is suspended by the floating hackle.

David points out another advantage of this technique. It can be tied very small and used as a midge pupa. With the white wing post sticking up above the hackle, it's easier to see the fly during the drift. As if that weren't enough, it also resembles a crippled dun that never quite made it to the surface film. And we all know how much trout like cripples.

Finally, by not tying off behind the eye you can finish the fly off anywhere on the hook. This means you can tie a smaller fly on a bigger hook and increase the odds of staying connected after the take.

## Tying Steps

1. Tie in a wing post of poly material. Start as you would to make spent wings, lift both ends, and wrap around the base to form the post.

2. Tie in the hackle by the butt end.

3. Advance the thread well past the bend.

4. Dub a rough body of hare's ear that ends just ahead of the wing post.

5. Dub a small thorax ahead of the wing post.

6. Leave the thread behind the wing post on the far side of the hook.

7. Wind the hackle around the post three or four times.

8. Wrap the thread clockwise under the hackle four times to secure it. Trim the excess hackle.

9. Tie the thread off under the hackle.

**MATERIALS**
Hook: Daiichi 1140, size 14
Thread: Brown, 8/0
Shuck: Olive-brown Z-lon
Body: Brown small D-Rib
Thorax: Brown Super Fine dubbing
Gill: White poly yarn

30

MZ's
EMERGING MIDGE
*Tied by Marc Zandell*

Marc Zandell of the Boulder Boat Works (www.boulderboatworks.com) in Colorado needed a more effective stillwater pattern for imitating midges so he developed his own. His approach is a good example of how we can all break out of a rut by paying attention to the details.

On his way to go fishing one day Marc realized that he was out of midge patterns, so he stopped in at a fly shop to buy a few. Unfortunately, they weren't very successful. Ever the resourceful angler, he caught a few naturals and returned to the tying bench to see what he could come up with. He tied this pattern to closely match what he saw on the water.

He reports that this is an especially durable fly. It's best fished in the first 6 feet of the water column. It can be stripped or still-fished on a 12-foot leader, and Marc goes heavy with a 3X tippet due to the large fish this fly seems to attract (including a 9-pound rainbow). You can cast the fly and allow it to sink naturally or add a split shot a foot or so above the fly. Be sure to use a large strike indicator. Marc also fishes this midge in tandem with a large Woolly Bugger. He figures it looks like something big chasing a nymph.

He's used the MZ's Emerging Midge in Colorado's Spinney Mountain Reservoir and in many mountain lakes from Utah to California. This pattern is most effective in early morning or late afternoon because that's when midges tend to hatch.

## Tying Steps

1. Lay down a thread base that extends well down the bend of the hook.

2. Tie in several strands of olive-brown Z-lon as a tail. Be sure the tail stands off the hook rather than pointing too far down toward the point.

3. Tie in the D-Rib and wind it forward to make a segmented body.

4. Dub a small thorax.

5. Add a small bunch of white poly for gills. Make sure it extends out over the hook eye.

6. Make a small head of thread, whip finish, and cement.

**MATERIALS**
  Hook: Daiichi 1270, sizes 16–22
  Thread: Brown, 8/0
  Tail: Brown partridge
  Body: Brown, small D-Rib
  Underbody: Brown or yellow thread, tapered
  Wing Case: Brown Medallion Sheeting
  Thorax: Brown Micro-Fly dubbing
  Legs: Brown partridge

## 31

STALCUP'S
BAETIS NYMPH
*Tied by Shane Stalcup*

Shane Stalcup (www.stalcupflies.com) is used to taking chances around the tying bench. It's how he makes his living. So when he comes up with a new pattern, flyfishers everywhere usually take notice. A close observation of *Baetis* led him to this technique for legging mayflies.

Shane had always tied his patterns with the legs emerging from the head, but when he looked closely at a natural he saw the legs emerging from the thorax. This simple observation has made a big difference in how he ties his flies. They now have a more natural profile that fish seem to key in on.

The first time this pattern got wet was on the Fryingpan River in Colorado. Shane and a friend were there a little ahead of the PMD hatch, so they worked the *Baetis* nymph to see what would happen. Shane was soon tied to a rainbow approaching 30 inches and the fly went on to produce well in normal hatch conditions, so there must be something to his new approach.

## TYING STEPS

1. Lay down a thread base.

2. Tie in a few partridge fibers for a tail.

3. Cut some D-Rib at an angle, so that when it's wrapped the curved side will be up. Tie it in at the tail.

4. Form a slightly tapered underbody of thread and then wrap the D-Rib over and forward. Start by stretching the first wraps of D-Rib and reduce the tension as you move forward.

5. Tie in the wing case material right behind the eye, but make sure it extends out over the eye.

6. Wrap a small amount of dubbing from the eye to the center of the thorax.

7. Cut the center stem from a partridge feather. Pull the feather through your fingers to even up the tips on a bundle of fibers. Measure the length of the tips from the hook eye to the middle of the hook. Tie the bundle parallel to the shank with the tips sticking out toward the front.

8. Dub the rest of the thorax back to where the wing case will be tied off.

9. Pull the wing case material back over the partridge, separating the fibers into legs. Tie the wing case down with two or three wraps, but don't trim it yet.

10. Advance the thread to the eye and tie off.

11. Go to the rear edge of the wing case and pull the excess sheeting sticking out the back while you trim it just beyond where it was tied down. You should end up with a V-cut, with each side of the "V" resembling a wing stub.

### Materials

Hook: Tiemco 100, sizes 16–18
Thread: Black, 8/0
Tail: Natural dun Betts Tailing Fibers
Rump Patch: Adams gray Antron
Abdomen and Thorax: Mahogany-red
    Umpqua Superfine dubbing
Wing: White Antron yarn

## 32

### Mataura Spinner
*Tied by Chris Dore*

I just never know how much to believe about fishing tales from New Zealand. There's always a lot of talk about how technical the fishing is, but then anglers seem to return home with all kinds of pictures of huge trout. Either there's a whole lot of monstrous trout for the catching, or there's a thriving take-your-picture-with-an-inflatable-fish industry down there.

Chris Dore of Trout Safaris (www.troutsafaris.co.nz) in Queenstown, New Zealand, knows a great deal about taking large trout, and the Mataura Spinner is one of his favorite flies. His only caution concerning this pattern is that it shouldn't be dressed too heavily. Only a small amount of poly is required to float the fly. Too heavy a dressing will often put down selective fish.

The Mataura River may be New Zealand's most famous brown trout fishery. The pool-riffle-pool configuration for almost its entire length means ideal habitat for massive populations of mayflies. Anglers from around the world come here in search of the ultimate match-the-hatch fishing for the adult stage of these insects.

The most selective fish are found in slow, glassy pools on the lower reaches of the river below Gore. It's here that the Mataura Spinner earned its reputation as a go-to fly. Chris notes that your success in these pools goes up if you abandon the upstream cast in favor of a downstream "snake" cast. This allows the drag-free fly to be the first thing that comes into the trout's window.

The spinner phase of the Mataura midge is responsible for the "mad Mataura rise," when astounding numbers of big browns feed almost recklessly. The spinners hover and then drop to the surface like tiny stones. Once the feeding trout are fixed on these spinners they'll take a spent-wing pattern, and multiple variations aren't really necessary. However, if the Mataura browns are feeding specifically on spent-wings and you don't have any, Chris says, "You might as well hit the pub."

## Tying Steps

1. Lay down a thread base, stopping at the bend of the hook.

2. Dub a small ball of gray Antron yarn at the bend.

3. Tie in two tailing fibers on each side of the ball. Keep them well splayed by taking turns of thread right up against the dubbing ball. Their length should be equal to the hook shank.

4. Create a slim, tapered body from the fur and stop three-quarters of the way up the shank.

5. Tie in spent wings perpendicular to the body. Secure with four or five figure-eight wraps so they remain flat.

6. Use the same dubbing to build up a thorax around the wings.

7. Make a small thread head, whip finish, and cement.

**33**

Old Faithful
*Tied by Joe Brenton*

## Materials

Hook: Mustad 9672, sizes 12–14
Thread: Black, 3/0 monocord or 6/0
  Uni-Thread
Tail: Medium blue dun hackle fibers
Body: Orange floss, #12
Rib: Small chartreuse wire
Wing: Single olive ringneck pheasant
  saddle feather
Hackle: Medium blue dun

Joe Brenton (www.theflyman.com) from Otis, Colorado, describes this pattern as an adaptation of an older fly that was first developed in the 1960s by Leslie Hinshaw, a rural postman from Meeker, Colorado. The original pattern was popular in the mid-seventies and was reputed to work well on Joe's favorite waters.

While researching this pattern, Joe had a conversation with Terry Nicholson of Anglers All in Littleton. Terry's shop is one of the few in the state that still stocks the original pattern. Terry had met Leslie and his family while backpacking in Colorado's Flat Tops Wilderness. He came upon them crawling the Old Faithful behind a water-filled casting bubble with spinning rods—and taking fish with almost every cast.

This fly's effectiveness can be attributed to the pheasant flat wing, which imparts unique action. It wiggles when retrieved or held in the current, which makes the fly "sail" rather than sink during pauses. The natural coloration is variegated, and it looks buggy. Joe has tried several other feathers for the wing, but the original works best.

The original pattern called for a body of dubbed olive fur. Joe's version uses orange floss, which creates a lighter, smaller body that sails more easily than the original.

Joe first fished his pattern in 1983 on North Delaney Butte Lake near Walden, Colorado. At that time, there was a large population of browns that ranged up to 6 pounds. Inch-long caddis hatched from late afternoon until well after dark, and large trout came up to chase them. He cast to a large boiling rise and started swimming the fly with 6- to 10-inch strips. On the third strip a heavy fish hit so hard that Joe broke the fly off. He quickly switched from 4X to 2X tippet. Joe's two remaining flies lasted six fish each before meeting the same fate. We should all be so lucky.

## TYING STEPS

1. Lay down a thread base to the bend.

2. Tie in floss and wire at the bend.

3. Wrap the floss forward to make a body.

4. Reverse wrap the ribbing forward.

5. Tie the wing on flat.

6. Tie in the hackle.

7. Take three turns.

8. Make a head, whip finish, and cement.

**Materials**
  Hook: Dry fly, 1XL, size 10
  Thread: Black, 8/0
  Tail: Deer body hair
  Body: Green closed-cell foam; palmered
    fiery brown saddle hackle
  Thorax: Peacock herl
  Wing: Deer hair
  Hackle: Brown saddle

**34**

Len's Stimulator
*Tied by Len Rich*

Len Rich runs Eagle Lake Lodge (www.fishinglabrador.com). The lodge is 60 miles south of Goose Bay, Labrador, and boasts large brook trout and even larger northern pike. A few years ago, Len was experimenting with foam materials of many types when he developed a fly called the Unsinkable Poly Bug. The wings were made of the foam used for cushioning furniture and electronics. Then he discovered closed-cell foam, often called Silly Foam, and started a whole new round of experiments.

His fly is basically a variation of the versatile Stimulator—one of those buggy-looking flies that can imitate everything from a caddis to a stonefly to a grasshopper. It turned out to be the best fly for the next two seasons at the lodge, accounting for a large number of trout in excess of 6 pounds.

Len's 12 years of guiding have taught him that fooling big trout in crystal-clear water requires a skillful presentation. Even these "wilderness" trout must be approached with care. His method for fishing this pattern is simple. He dead-drifts the fly on an upstream cast. When fishing quieter water, he recommends twitching the fly a few feet and then stopping. Apparently, this gives the impression of an insect struggling to escape the water, and it often triggers a strike.

## Tying Steps

1. Lay down a thread base to the hook bend.

2. Tie in a small bunch of deer hair, making a short tail. Leave the butt ends along the length of the hook shank to improve buoyancy.

3. Tie in a fiery brown hackle by the tip to be used later for palmering.

4. Cut a thin strip of closed-cell foam from a sheet. Attach one end at the tail and wrap forward to create a body. Wrap tightly as you advance the foam. Stop one-third to one-quarter of the way to the eye. Tie off the body and trim.

5. Palmer the hackle forward over the foam, making five or six turns. Tie off, but don't trim.

6. Tie in a wing of deer hair back over the body, extending it to the tip of the tail. Trim the butt ends.

7. Tie in a piece of peacock herl at the wing base and wrap it forward four or five turns to the back of the eye. Leave the thread hanging behind the eye.

8. Grasp the remainder of the brown hackle and wrap it four or five times over the peacock herl.

9. Trim the hackle and make a head.

**MATERIALS**
Hook: Daiichi 1150, sizes 10–18
Thread: Danville 6/0, color to match naturals
Body: Light yellow Ice Dub
Shell: Softex
Feelers/Back Legs: Ostrich herl tips
Segmentation: Palmered ostrich herl
Eyes: Black permanent marker

**35**

**KolANdA's
BTS Scud**
*Tied by Rob Kolanda*

Rob Kolanda works for Rocky Mountain Anglers (www.rockymtanglers.com) in Boulder, Colorado, where he teaches the beginning fly-tying and fly-fishing classes. He also guides anglers on nearby waters and is the shop's Alaska and lake specialist. His BTS (Better Than Sex) series of flies has accounted for a lot of trout in recent years.

Rob was looking for a scud pattern that was not only effective, but that also could stand up to punishment from fish after fish. He developed this pattern after watching live scuds in an aquarium he keeps atop his tying desk. The captive scuds were a valuable resource because he was able to create a fly that has the nearly clear exoskeleton of the natural while showing the segmentation underneath. The Ice Dub provides subtle flash.

The BTS Scud has proven deadly in stillwaters, tailwaters, and spring creeks. Is it really better than sex? You'll have to decide for yourself.

## Tying Steps

1. Lay down a thread base to the bend of the hook.

2. Tie in ostrich herl tips at the bend for legs/feelers.

3. Tie in two longer ostrich herl fibers behind the feelers.

4. Dub a body and wrap back to the eye.

6. Tie in ostrich herl tips with the ends toward the hook point.

7. Palmer the herl from the bend back over the body to the hook eye.

8. Use a dubbing brush to force the herl and Ice Dub down.

9. Apply Softex to the back and allow it to dry.

10. Use permanent black marker to make small eyes on either side of the Softex at the bend (head of the fly).

**MATERIALS**
Hook: Standard dry fly, sizes 10–20
Thread: Gray or black, 8/0
Tail: Grizzly hackle fibers or gray
    Microfibetts
Wings: Grizzly hackle-point wings,
    preferably burnt or cut to shape
Body Humps: Black rabbit fur dubbing
Hackles: Dry fly; one grizzly, one brown

## 36

### ADAMANT
*Tied by Tom Brtalik*

Tom Brtalik of Tom's Fly-Fishing Service (www.tomsflyfishing.com) in New Cumberland, Pennsylvania, started thinking about a hybrid pattern that would combine the best characteristics of two effective flies—the Adams and the ant. A lot of tiers have tried to do this very thing, but few have succeeded so well.

Both the Adams and ant patterns seem to have silhouettes and colors that trout respond to. After a little experimentation, Tom came up with a pattern that now has a valued spot in his fly box.

Tom fishes the Adamant as a searching pattern, a terrestrial, or an attractor. In his experience, the wings and hackle provide great visibility on the water, while the brown and grizzly hackles create a very natural color.

In certain situations, the fly's effectiveness can be improved upon by trimming a small "V" in the bottom of the hackle. This allows the fly to float flush in the surface film, providing a cleaner silhouette. A good variation of this pattern includes cinnamon rabbit fur instead of black, particularly in the smaller sizes. You can also use hair wings in place of hackle points to improve flotation and visibility in fast water.

## Tying Steps

1. Tie in three or four hook-eye lengths behind the eye and spiral wrap sparsely to the beginning of the bend.

2. Tie in six to eight grizzly hackle fibers or gray Microfibetts for the tail. The tail length should equal the length of the entire hook, including the eye.

3. Spiral wrap the thread back to the original tie-in point. Tie in hackle-point wings, which should be the length of the shank only.

4. Spiral wrap (sparsely) the thread to the base of the tail. Dub black rabbit fur on the thread and wind the dubbing to form the rear body hump.

5. Spiral wrap the thread to three hook-eye lengths behind the base of the wing, leaving room to tie in the hackles. Dub the rabbit fur and wind a second body hump. Be sure to leave a visible space between the humps.

6. Tie in one grizzly hackle and one brown hackle behind the wings, with the shinny sides facing toward the rear of the hook.

7. Wind the brown hackle three or four turns behind the wing, then two or three turns in front of the wing, and tie off.

8. Wind the grizzly hackle in the same fashion on top of the brown hackle, taking care not to trap any of the brown fibers as you wind forward.

9. Tie off the grizzly hackle and whip finish the head.

## Materials

Hook: TMC 5236, sizes 2–8

Thread: Yellow, UTC 70 or 8/0

Head: Gold tungsten cone, sized to the hook

Tail: Cream marabou (optional: a few strands of pearl UV Ice Wing or Krystal Flash)

Body: Light yellow UV Ice Dub, picked out

Hackle: Light cream Metz saddle hackle

Rib: Fine gold Largartun wire

Collar: Light cream or beige hen neck or hen back

# 37

## Collier's Vanilla Ice Bugger

*Tied by Dennis Collier*

This enticing fly is a favorite of Dennis Collier of Rocky Mountain Anglers (www.rockymtanglers.com) in Boulder, Colorado. The original Vanilla Ice recipe is shown here, but a few excellent color variations have been developed in recent years, and they all catch big fish equally well. My favorite is the root beer and brandy.

Dennis created this pattern several years ago, but it sat forgotten in a remote corner of his fly box. While fishing Colorado's "Dream Stream," a section of the South Platte River between Spinney and Eleven Mile Reservoirs, Dennis was drawing a blank. Finally, after trying several patterns, he spotted the Vanilla Ice Bugger in his box. Big fish began slamming the fly immediately and it saved the day—along with countless subsequent days. Now it's Dennis's pattern of choice when fishing most moving water.

Dennis even fishes this pattern during hatches. He believes that fish are opportunistic feeders. When bugs are on the water, small forage fish will also be actively feeding, and a big predator trout has a tough time saying no to a mouthful of meat that has carelessly exposed itself. Dennis notes that the Dream Stream is known as a midge and *Baetis* tailwater fishery. He seldom, if ever, sees another angler fishing streamers on this section. If only they knew what they were missing!

The blond/brown color combination of this fly is so popular with Dennis's clients that he ties it exclusively for Rocky Mountain Anglers. So if you want to buy one instead of tying your own, you'll have to contact the fly shop.

## Tying Steps

1. Slide a cone head up to the hook eye.

2. Lay down a thread base to the bend.

3. Tie in a tail of marabou equal to the length of the hook shank.

4. Tie in wire for the rib.

5. Tie in a saddle hackle for palmering.

6. Dub and wrap a body of Ice Dub right up to the cone head. Pick it out to soften the profile.

7. Palmer the saddle hackle over the body to the cone head.

8. Counter-wrap the wire over the body and palmered hackle.

9. Tie in a hen neck hackle behind the cone head and wrap a collar.

10. Whip finish and cement.

**Materials**
Hook: Cabela's Model 2, size 12 barbless
Thread: Black, 14/0 (to reduce buildup)
Body: True blue poly wool, half a strand
Hackle: Grizzly, oversized for a size 12
hook

## 38

### Blue Damsel
*Tied by John Kowalski*

Extended-body flies look great, but tying them so that they are rugged enough to stand up to some abuse is another matter. Here's an easy, durable, and effective technique for damsels from Nevada guide John Kowalski (775-782-6576 or jack@pobox.com). It sounds complex, but ties easily and lasts for more than just one hookup.

He fishes the Blue Damsel for rainbows on ponds and lakes and encourages his clients to use a 3X tippet because the strikes can be downright vicious.

## TYING STEPS

1. Start with a pin or needle clamped in the vise. You'll build the body on this and then transfer it to the hook (see inset photo).

2. Separate half a strand of poly wool, 3 inches long.

3. Tie just a few wraps of thread near the point of the pin, creating a non-slip base.

4. Tie in the poly wool over these wraps, making sure the poly stays on top of the needle. Leave the ends long to serve as a thorax and post for parachute hackles.

5. Use 6 to 10 close wraps to make a dark band.

6. Use a large spiral wrap to move the thread ⅛ inch toward the vise, leaving a blue band.

7. Repeat this process, making alternating black and blue bands to create a 1-inch-long body.

8. Reverse the tying direction, heading back toward the point by making five turns of thread over each original black band, and ending where you started.

9. Whip finish, cut off, and liberally cement every wrap. The body should be 60-percent blue, 40-percent black—and thin.

10. Slip the wool off the pin.

11. Put a hook in the vise and lay down a thread base from the eye to the bend.

12. Tie the body in at the bend with the long ends pointing toward the eye and the extended body sticking out past the bend.

13. Use a large wrap to move the thread to the middle of the shank and firmly tie the loose ends down.

14. Take large wraps to move the thread to just behind the eye, but without binding the loose poly wool down.

15. Cement all wraps.

16. Pull the poly wool over the wraps to the eye and tie firmly. Move the thread to the bend.

17. Fold the poly back over and tie in at the bend. Raise the poly and take wraps under the tie-in point, creating a parachute post.

18. Wrap the hackle parachute-style, six turns, then tie and cut off the excess. Trim the post to length.

19. Use large wraps to bring the thread to the eye. Make a small head and whip finish.

20. Cement the wraps that show under the hook.

**MATERIALS**
Hook: TMC 2487, sizes 16–18
Thread: Black, 8/0
Bead: Black, ³⁄₃₂ or 2mm
Body: Brassie-sized blue wire
Collar: Stalcup's Microfine
Dry Fly Dubbing, Trico

## 39

Quad B
*Tied by Stan Benton*

B lue. Now there's a color tiers seldom add to their nymph patterns, although maybe it's time to reconsider. Stan Benton, manager and guide at Angler's Covey (www.anglerscovey.com) in Colorado Springs, Colorado, has been working with the color blue for the past decade. He does this because blue is supposed to be the most visible color underwater. He's also read some research claiming that trout will take a blue-dyed salmon egg over any other color, regardless of the background color. So he began incorporating blue into some of his subsurface patterns.

The Quad B was designed to suggest a caddis larva. The first time Stan fished this fly was in the spring on the Arkansas River near Cotopaxi. He began in a nice-looking stretch of water with patterns that had previously been effective, but picked up only one fish. Then he went back to the top of the run and tried the new Quad B pattern. He immediately started catching fish, landing at least a dozen. And this pattern has continued to fish well. It's especially effective on freestone streams that have good caddis populations, and it seems to work best when fished along the bottom.

As for naming his flies, Stan admits he often finds this task difficult. Since the pattern is essentially a black beadhead blue Brassie, he thought "Quad B" would be most appropriate. Creative or uncreative names aside, this fly is worth adding to your arsenal.

## Tying Steps

1. Slide a bead up to the hook eye.

2. Lay down a thread base to the bend of the hook.

3. Tie in a length of Brassie-sized blue wire.

4. Advance the thread to the bead and then wrap the wire forward to form the body.

5. Dub a collar about the same diameter and size as the bead.

### Materials

Hook: Tiemco 200R or Daiichi 1270, sizes 6–10
Thread: Brown, 6/0
Tail: Dark brown marabou
Body: Dark brown dubbing mixed with orange
 Antron and copper-colored Lite-Brite
Sticks: Pheasant tail fibers
Collar: Dirty yellow Antron or rabbit dubbing
Legs: Black hen hackle
Head: Gold, copper, or black bead
Weight: Lead wire, .015

## 40

### Bill's Stick Caddis
*Tied by Bill Carnazzo*

Ever see those giant October Caddis lurking around in western streams? Bill Carnazzo from Spring Creek Flycraft and Guide Service (916-663-2604) in Newcastle, California, actually studied these mega-caddis and developed a fly to imitate them during the autumn emergence. When the caddis are at their largest the trout eat them like candy, and this is the perfect pattern to take advantage of it.

Bill likes to fish this fly on a short line using the traditional high-stick technique for nymphing. He recommends working carefully through any section where the water flow slows down: on seams, behind rocks, below small falls, or anyplace an obstruction might provide a hiding place for fish. His secret is to keep the fly on the bottom as long as possible on each drift.

And remember, the first cast to any location is always the most likely to bring a strike, so stay in touch with your fly because the take may be very light.

## Tying Steps

1. Slide a bead up to the hook eye.

2. Wrap lead wire 15 to 20 times around the shank and force the bead against the eye.

3. Secure lead with thread, and then wrap a thread base back to a spot directly above the barb.

4. Make a small ¼-inch-long tail of marabou fibers.

5. Form a dubbing loop at the bend, and then move the bobbin to the midpoint of the shank.

6. Dub a loop body and wrap it to the midpoint of the shank.

7. Tie in four pheasant tail fibers parallel to the hook so that the thread divides the fibers in half lengthwise.

8. Spread the rear-facing fibers around the top half of the hook and tie off.

9. Take the forward-facing pheasant fibers, one by one, and pull them back and down so they also point toward the bend, but on the bottom half of the shank. Tie them off.

10. Repeat steps 5 through 9 to make the forward half of the body. Leave an ⅛-inch space for a collar. Building the body in this manner allows the pheasant fibers to stick out of the middle and forward end of the body.

11. Spin on a collar of yellow dubbing.

12. Add nymph-style legs.

13. Whip finish.

### Materials

Hook: TMC 102Y, sizes 16–22
Thread: Color to match natural, 8/0
Abdomen: Two pieces of Ultra Wire, one light, one dark
Wing Post: Poly yarn in white, high-vis red, yellow, or green
Body and Thorax: Extra fine dubbing to match the lighter Ultra Wire
Hackle: Grizzly

## 41

### Ultra Emerger
*Tied by Pat Higgins*

Pat Higgins, owner and head guide of the Bear Creek Fly Fishing Company (www.bearcreekflyfishing.com) in Idledale, Colorado, wanted a good emerger and slow-water fly. He found that a Kinkhammer-style pattern was successful everywhere he fished. The only problem was that in the smaller sizes—18 to 24—the sunken abdomen effect of the Kinkhammer didn't work well. It wasn't heavy enough to sink the abdomen into the surface film, so the fly didn't behave like a natural would.

When Wapsi came out with Ultra Wire, Pat began experimenting. It worked so well he adopted the "Ultra" to name a series of flies, including this emerger. The bend in the hook is what makes this pattern so deadly. Even in midge sizes, the fly sits well down in the surface film like an emerger.

Pat says he was fishing the Fall River in central Oregon some time ago when a nice rainbow broke off his Ultra Emerger. He tied on another and the same thing happened. Down to his last one, Pat finally landed a 16-inch rainbow. He knew it was the same fish because he also retrieved his other two flies from the fish's mouth. Now that's a fish story!

## Tying Steps

1. Using a fine-point set of needle-nose pliers, place a 30- to 40-degree bend in the hook shank about one-quarter the shank length back from the eye.

2. Place the hook in your vise with the long end of the shank parallel to the bench top.

3. Cut two pieces of colored wire (one light, one dark) about 3 to 4 inches long. Wrap both pieces around the hook together. Keep them parallel, just like you would on a Brassie; don't allow the wires to become twisted around each other. Wrap from the hook bend to the bend you made, which gives the body a barber-pole look. Use your fingernail to push the wire tight. Trim off the ends of the wire and secure with Super Glue.

4. Adjust the hook in the vise so that the front, or small, end of the shank is now parallel with the bench.

5. Tie in the material for the wing post in the center of this short-shank area. Create a post as you would on any parachute pattern. (Pat ties in the poly yarn by folding it up and around the shank and then securing it with a figure-eight thread wrap.)

6. Attach your hackle and wrap parachute-style, with only two or three turns. Secure.

7. Dub the body and thorax with a fine dubbing that matches the lighter-colored wire. In sizes 20 and smaller, use thread rather than dubbing to form the body.

8. Form a small head, whip finish, and cement.

**MATERIALS**
Hook: Any streamer hook, size 6–10
Thread: Black and dark green, 4/0
Weight: Nontoxic lead wire
Tail: Peacock herl
Body: Black plush material, shredded
Legs: Black hen hackle

## 42

FALLON SLAYER
*Tied by Dan Fallon*

Here's a stonefly pattern developed by guide Dan Fallon (415-332-3803 or www.fallonfly.com) from Sausalito, California. Dan is definitely from the "big fish want big flies" school.

He prefers to fish this fly with quick tugs under and around ledges and stream edges. By fishing it this way he hopes to stimulate what he calls an "alien invasion" strike. Another method he recommends is to bounce the Fallon Slayer off the top of a flat rock to surprise waiting fish. (Given the size of this fly, they might be striking out of self-defense.)

The Slayer looks like it was tied during the second week of a fly-tying school, but Dan has been guiding too long to be concerned with how a fly looks to anglers. He just wants a fly he knows the fish will eat. That's what so great about guide flies: They may look too simple to be effective, but their results can't be denied.

So where does plush body material come from? Dan looks in old clothing stores for any chenille-like fabric he can shred to make a buggy wrapping. Old women's hats, purses, and vests from the 1930s and '40s provide lots of materials worth trying.

## Tying Steps

1. Wrap a few turns of nontoxic lead wire close to the eye.

2. Secure the lead with thread and lay down a thread base to the bend of the hook.

3. Tie in two strands of peacock herl as tails. Make the tails as long as the body.

4. Let the butt ends extend over the shank and past the eye ½ inch for feelers.

5. Wrap a fat, cigar-shaped body of black plush with a taper at each end.

6. Tie in some green thread at the tail for the rear segment. Wrap it right over the rear body taper and tie it off.

7. At the forward edge of the body, tie in an extra-long hen hackle and wrap it over the forward end of the body.

8. Trim the hackles off the top of the body, leaving legs on the sides and bottom.

9. Make a head and tie off.

**43**

Hare and Peacock
*Tied by Jack Pangburn*

Materials
Hook: Mustad 3906B, sizes 8–18
Thread: Black
Weight (optional): Lead-free wire
Tail: Coachman red hackle fibers (light
gray yarn for an emerger)
Rib: Gold oval tinsel
Body: PrismFlash mixed with
iridescent peacock SLF
Wing: Rabbit or hare
Head: Black, lacquered, and shaped

W hen this fly first arrived, I misread the name and thought it was the Hairy Peacock. But Jack Pangburn (www.flytyingworld.com) from Westbury, New York, had something else in mind. He's a guide, tier, and artist who wanted to develop a life-like caddis pupa wet fly. "Life-like" for Jack means fibers that pulsate and appear to breathe. For trout, this action transforms an object into something edible.

Jack knows that when caddis pupae swim toward the surface they are an easy meal, and because they are so numerous, emerging pupae are a primary food source for fish. However, relatively few fly tiers tie caddis pupa patterns. Also, few of the patterns in use actually look like a swimming caddis pupa.

After much tinkering with hackle, dubbing, colors, hook sizes, weight, beads, and wing material, the Hare and Peacock was born. The body must have a definite pear shape, with the widest portion of the abdomen over the weighted wire. The rabbit fur, with guard hair left in, gives the Hare and Peacock the illusion of life.

The version shown here—with gray-tan natural rabbit fur and peacock dubbing—is by far the best producer of the various color combinations. Larger flies may be tied up to 1¼ inches long, while the smallest run only ¼ inch. Jack suggests tying up a few with the weight at the bend of the hook. This makes the fly swim with the tail down, just as the naturals do.

## Tying Steps

1. Wrap thread to the bend and tie in the hackle fibers for the tail (or yarn shuck, if tying a floating version).

2. Tie in a length of gold oval tinsel to be used as a rib.

3. For the sinking version, add several wraps of lead-free wire.

4. Give the wire and thread wraps a coat of cement.

5. Spin some dubbing and wrap a body. Stop well behind the eye to leave room for the bulky wing.

6. Wind the tinsel forward to rib the body and tie off.

7. To make a wing, cut a bunch of rabbit fur close to the hide, capturing underfur as well as guard hairs.

8. Position the rabbit fur so it extends a little beyond the tail (or to the midpoint of the yarn shuck).

9. Trim the butt ends of the wing and work cement into the fiber ends.

10. Build a round head, whip finish, and cement.

11. Finish with black lacquer.

**MATERIALS**

Hook: Mustad 9671 or 9672, 2X long, sizes 8–12
Weight (optional): Several turns of lead wire
Thread: Black, 6/0
Tail: White rabbit
Butt: Red chenille
Body: White chenille
Collar: White hen or saddle hackle

**44**

WHITE RABBIT
*Tied by Bill Strout*

I t's not always easy to catch fish, but when you're a guide your clients expect it to happen regardless of the conditions. This doesn't reflect poorly on clients: it's just a fact of life. They're paying for your expertise and you'd better measure up. Here's a "down and dirty" fly that guide Bill Strout relies on when the going gets tough.

Bill is from the Green Mountain Guide Service (fishmaine@panax.com or 207-288-4050) in Bar Harbor, Maine. He told me he's been fishing this fly for 20 years. It was originally designed as an attractor pattern, which may explain the often-used color combination of red and white. Aside from Daredevil lures, I can't think of another swimming thing that has this color combination. But you can't argue with success.

He uses this fly primarily for trout and landlocked salmon, and you can bet that if it didn't produce consistently he'd have quit going to it years ago. He's also done well with it on bass and perch in stillwaters large and small. With a species list like that, there must be something fundamentally attractive about the color and action. As a matter of fact, white seems to turn up often as an attractor color.

Bill fishes the White Rabbit wet and prefers to retrieve it slowly along the bottom with a stop-and-go motion. This technique is especially effective in slow stretches of rivers and backwaters with almost no water movement. Bill says it's the rabbit fur that makes the fly work so well. The slow pulsing motion gives the fur plenty of time to do its enticing Dance of the Thousand Veils.

## TYING STEPS

1. After laying down a thread base, tie in a tail of white rabbit fur, using both guard hairs and underfur.

2. Create a butt with two wraps of red chenille and tie off.

3. Tie in white chenille up against the red and wrap a body forward toward the eye.

4. Make a collar of two or three wraps of white hen hackle or a small saddle hackle.

5. Wrap a head, whip finish, and cement.

## Materials

Hook: Any model, 3X long with a slightly curved
    shank, sizes 6–14
Thread: Light rust or color to match body, 6/0
Tail: Elk or deer hair
Body: Antron matched to the color of the naturals
Rib: Fine wire or thread
Underwing: Calf tail the same color as the body
Overwing: Elk hair
Post: White closed-cell foam
Hackle: Dry-fly quality, matched to body color
Legs: Fine-diameter rubber

## 45

### Parachute Stonefly
*Tied by Pat Pierson*

P at Pierson from Rocky Fork Outfitters (www.redlodge.com/rockyforkoutfitters or 406-445-2598) in Red Lodge, Montana, must be one tough hombre. He notes that this fly is sometimes called the Dead Baby Hummingbird. Imagine telling that to some 10-year-old kid on her first fishing trip.

Pat developed this pattern years ago by borrowing various attributes from several conventional stonefly patterns. His fly floats high in the fast water where big golden stoneflies are found (not to mention big trout). The white post provides great visibility, making it easier to track the fly in broken water. And the rubber legs seem to excite even reluctant fish.

The buoyancy of this fly is also perfect for floating a dropper fly. This method of fishing a nymph, or even two, under a dry fly has been popular for quite some time. The problem is that the dropper often sinks the dry fly before the drift ends. With this particular pattern, there's no need to worry about how big the dropper fly is. Pat claims it'll float a spark plug. While car parts won't catch many fish, it's still good to know you can keep this fly on the surface all day long.

## TYING STEPS

1. After laying down a thread base, tie in a very short tail of elk or deer hair. The hairs should be flared to the sides to add extra buoyancy, and this can be accomplished by finishing the tail with a tight tying loop.

2. Tie in a length of fine wire or thread for ribbing.

3. Dub Antron and form a thick body two-thirds of the way toward the eye. Leave plenty of room for the rest of the materials to follow.

4. Rib the body with wire. This improves durability and segments the body.

5. Tie in the parachute post up against the front of the body.

6. Tie in an underwing of calf tail the same color as the body and extend it slightly beyond the tail.

7. Place an overwing of elk hair on top of the calf tail and make it slightly shorter.

8. Tie in two sets of rubber legs in front of the post.

9. Tie in two dry-fly hackles behind the post, wrap them around it, and tie off in front. Fast-water flies require more hackle wraps than slow-water flies.

10. Dub more body material and cover the remainder of the hook.

11. Make a small head and finish it off.

## MATERIALS

Hook: Tiemco 3769 or 5262, 1X heavy and
2–3X long, sizes 6–12
Thread: Black, 6/0, and red, 8/0, unwaxed
Body: Mylar, coated with Zap-A-Gap
Wings: Two pairs of guinea hen, dyed olive
or natural
Eyes: Mylar strip
Gill Band: Red thread

**46**

LOEBERG
*Tied by Tom Loe*

The Loeberg is the creation of Tom Loe from Sierra Drifters in Mammoth Lakes, California (www.sierradrifters.com). He designed this trout pattern to imitate perch fry in large reservoirs in the foothills of the Sierra Nevadas.

Tom fishes this fly with all types of lines, depending on the conditions. He's discovered that good results require varied retrieves during each cast in order to imitate the erratic swimming motion of the natural fry. He likes to work the fly around weed beds and drop-offs, and he casts directly toward the shoreline from his boat rather than parallel to it.

Trolling works occasionally, but the best success comes from working the fly at various depths with a lot of motion. Perch fry move quickly and erratically, usually with many pauses in between. They tend to school up around weed beds and shallow shoreline areas during low-light periods. The retrieves Tom recommends bring violent strikes, so be prepared to keep your rod tip up and let the line play out freely.

The construction and profile of Tom's Loeberg is similar to that of the Hornberg, a famous old trout fly from the East Coast. It's common to start out fishing the Hornberg on a dead drift as a dry fly, and then retrieve it as a wet fly. This essentially allows you to show the fish two flies during each cast. I suspect this would work with the Loeberg, too.

## Tying Steps

1. Lay down a thread base to a point directly above the hook barb.

2. Tie in silver Mylar and wrap back toward the eye, stopping one-third of the distance to the eye.

3. Tie off and coat with Zap-A-Gap to reinforce the Mylar.

4. Tie in two guinea hen feathers, with the curves matched so one fits inside the other, on the far side of the hook. The feather tips should extend three or four times the length of the hook shank. The sides should be symmetrical and lay flat against the body.

5. Repeat the process with another pair of guinea feathers on the near side.

6. Tie in strips of Mylar on both sides as eyes. As an alternative, you could use jungle cock or even short pieces of Krystal Flash.

7. Wind a full collar of grizzly hackle.

8. Create a head and whip finish.

9. Make a red gill band of thread behind the eye.

10. Whip finish and cement the head.

**MATERIALS**
Hook: Tiemco 2457 (scud hook), size 18
Thread: Gray, 8/0
Head: Small pearl bead
Tail: Pheasant tail fibers
Rib: Fine silver wire
Back Strap: Pheasant tail fibers
Flashback: Krystal Flash
Abdomen: Muskrat fur
Thorax: Muskrat fur

## 47

GREG'S EMERGER
*Tied by Greg Cunningham*

B ack in 1994, Greg Cunningham, national sales manager for Brookside Flies (www.brooksideflies.com), wanted a *Baetis* nymph for use on Colorado's South Platte River. Greg, who also guides for Trout Trips (www.trouttrips. com), says he designed this imitation to effectively imitate the very small bugs finicky fish here seem to like.

Greg first fished this pattern with great results during the spring and fall *Baetis* hatches. Later, he learned that it was also useful during winter as a small midge pupa in sizes 22–24. After fishing the original gray color for a couple of years, Greg decided to expand the variations to include black (Trico), yellow (PMD), and olive (another BWO).

The Greg's Emerger has worked well throughout Colorado and on waters from the San Juan River in New Mexico to the Rush River in Wisconsin. It has become a mainstay on the Grey Reef section of the North Platte in Wyoming.

## TYING STEPS

1. Slip a small pearl bead onto the hook.

2. Tie in three pheasant tail fibers for the tail, cocking them slightly downward. Do not trim the tag ends. Instead, secure them with thread and use them later for the back strap.

3. Tie in fine silver wire for ribbing.

4. Dub an abdomen of muskrat fur. Advance the dubbing three-quarters of the way up the shank.

5. Pull the tag ends of the pheasant tail over the back of the abdomen to create a back strap.

6. Advance the silver wire to rib the abdomen.

7. At the forward end of the abdomen, tie in Krystal Flash for the flashback.

8. Dub a thorax of muskrat fur slightly fatter than the abdomen.

9. Pull the Flash over the thorax and tie off behind the bead.

## Materials

Hook: TMC 2488 or equivalent, sizes 14–20
Thread: Color to match body, 6/0
Bead: Gold to match hook: $^3\!/_{32}$ on size 14, $^5\!/_{64}$ on size 16, etc.
Body: Antron dubbing such as Orvis or Wapsi Life Cycle in light brown, tan, or dark olive
Rib: Fine gold wire

## 48

### Quick and Easy Beadhead Nymph
*Tied by Randy Romig*

Anytime I hear the words "quick and easy" I pay attention. Randy Romig of Triple R Fly Fishing Guide Service (www.triplertroutguides.com) out of Barto, Pennsylvania, is a man after my own heart. He tried more complicated beadhead patterns back when beads first became available, but what he really wanted was a simple and effective fly that would reduce his time at the bench. His early versions included fox squirrel for the dubbing, but it didn't seem to hold up as well as Antron.

Randy always fishes this fly with a strike indicator, and he adds a small split shot 8 to 12 inches above the fly to get it down deep. He fishes the rig straight upstream or up and across, but always on a dead drift. In slower pools he gives it a small twitch as it nears the end of the drift. The twitch makes the fly look as if it's hatching, which often elicits a strike from reluctant trout.

He ties the Quick and Easy Beadhead Nymph in sizes 14 through 20, but uses the size 14 around 80 percent of the time. When he fishes streams that see lots of angling pressure, he'll drop down to the smaller sizes.

Tied in the colors and sizes recommended by Randy, this fly covers the entire fishing season and country because it suggests many different types of naturals. For this reason, it often out-fishes Pheasant Tails and Hare's Ears that are more suggestive of specific nymphs. In fact, Randy uses this pattern year-round. His clients often tell him they are amazed at the effectiveness of this simple fly. They usually ask him to tie a dozen for them to fish on their home waters.

## Tying Steps

1. Pinch down the barb and slide on a bead.

2. Tie in thread behind the bead to force it up against the eye, and then wind halfway to the bend.

3. Tie in fine gold wire.

4. Continue making turns of thread to the bend, wrapping over the wire.

5. Dub and wrap a slightly tapered body up to the bead.

6. Rib with gold wire and tie off behind the bead.

7. Finish with a drop of cement.

**MATERIALS**
Hook: Mustad 9672, size 6–8
Thread: Black, 6/0
Tail: Red hackle fibers
Underbody: Yellow poly yarn
Rib: Brown dry-fly hackle
Underwing: Golden pheasant tippets
Overbody: Tan foam cut to shape
Legs: Orange rubber legs
Collar: Brown dry-fly hackles

**49**

KILLAHOPPER
*Tied by Dan Hurzeler*

The Killahopper looks like it evolved from the best parts of several different flies. But don't let its looks turn you off because this fly has a way of turning on trout in the Henry's Fork, the South Fork of the Snake, and the Madison River. It's the invention of Dan Hurzeler, who owns Fin Chasers (208-557-0333) in Idaho Falls, Idaho.

This is Dan's go-to fly when hoppers are on the water, but the trout aren't taking them readily. It's not a finesse fly. He says the Killahopper should be fished in fairly shallow water and cast hard so it hits with a splat. As soon as it lands, he recommends stripping the line to make the fly jump. This quick move calls even more attention to the fly. Dan believes the success of this fly lies in its silhouette and the disturbance it creates when worked aggressively.

His first experience with the Killahopper, however, resulted in a 3-pound whitefish. Although Dan wasn't too happy, the other guys he was fishing with got a good laugh. He kept fishing with it, though, and the results soon showed that this is definitely one fly worth trying for larger trout in shallow water.

So next time the hoppers are on the water, get out there and thrash the surface with a Killahopper—you never know what will show up.

## Tying Steps

1. At the bend of the hook, tie in red hackle for a tail.

2. Tie in a brown hackle for ribbing and a piece of yellow poly yarn, both at the point where you tied the tail.

3. Wind the poly forward only as far as the middle of the hook shank. Leave lots of room for the forward hackle.

4. Palmer the brown hackle forward to the end of the poly body and tie off.

5. Tie in golden pheasant tippets as an underwing just to the front of the body. Be sure to splay them out to each side.

6. Tie in two brown dry-fly hackles at the forward end of the poly body.

7. Tie a tan foam overbody on top of the hook, also in front of the poly yarn.

8. Tie two sets of rubber legs on top of the foam body. These should extend twice the length of the foam.

9. Take several turns of brown hackle over the foam body (where it's tied in) and between the rubber legs.

10. Wrap the remainder of the first hackle and the entire second hackle around the hook shank up to the eye, but underneath the foam body.

11. Make a head and cement.

## Materials

Hook: Any 2X heavy and 2X long wet/nymph
hook, sizes 8–22 (sizes 10 and 12 are best)
Thread: Black, 3/0 or 6/0
Weight (optional): Lead wire
Dubbing Loop: Stainless steel, .005-inch, or a
single strand of filament from speaker wire
or lamp cord
Abdomen: Natural fur
Thorax: Beaver or muskrat
Hackle: Grouse or woodcock body feather

**50**

WIRED WONDER
*Tied by Bill Strapko*

Just when you think you've seen it all, something unusual sneaks right up on you. The tying method for this fly from Bill Strapko of the Connecticut Yankee Guide Service (wstrapko@hotmail.com) is something I've never seen before. It may have been around for some time, but it's new to me. Bill describes the Wired Wonder as an adaptation of a Sylvester Nemes soft-hackle pattern. The advantage of his method is that it creates a durable, bombproof fly.

Bill ties this fly in three colors: creamy tan, natural rabbit, and buggy green. On some Connecticut waters, no weight can be used except for what is built into the fly, so he ties his weighted flies with brown thread instead of black so he can quickly identify each type.

He relates that this is a nondiscriminating fly. While he likes rabbit, gray squirrel, opossum, or woodchuck, he'll use almost any unfortunate road kill for the body. If you decide to make your own roadside pickup, just be sure to approach it from upwind. I thought he was kidding about this method of collecting materials until I challenged him to "collect" a woodchuck we saw in a cornfield next to the road we were driving on. I still haven't recovered from that event.

## TYING STEPS

1. Lay down a thread base to the bend.

2. Tie in a long dubbing loop of wire and return the thread to the bend.

3. Wax the thread and dub on the fur.

4. Catch the thread inside the wire loop about halfway down, and twist it together. Not too tight, though, or the wire will break. Make just enough twists to hide the wire in the fur.

5. Wind the dubbing forward about two-thirds of the way to the eye.

6. Tie off the dubbing loop.

7. Dub in fur for a thicker thorax and repeat step 4, using the remainder of the wire dubbing loop.

8. Wind forward, leaving room for the hackle and head.

9. Prepare a hackle feather by holding it from the tip and stroking the fibers back, making them stand out away from the stem.

10. Tie in the hackle by the tip and take two or three turns.

11. Hold the fibers back, and then add several turns of thread up against the thorax so the fibers point toward the bend.

12. Wind a head, whip finish, and cement.

**Materials**
Hook: Barbless dry fly, sizes 14–18
Thread: Black, 6/0
Body: Black Fly-Rite
Shell: White poly yarn

## 51

Dräpar'n
*Tied by Dennis Damm*

**D**ennis Damm, owner of Älvdalens Fiskecenter (www.alvdalenfiske.com) in Sweden, sent along what he describes as his best summer-night fly. Translated from Swedish, Dräpar'n means "the slayer." I'm willing to bet more than just a few kronor that it will slay some fish for you, too. It's a simple-to-tie and suggestive fly that should work well virtually anywhere.

Dennis developed this fly a couple of years ago when he could see fish rising but couldn't identify what they were taking. However, from the rise forms it was obvious the bugs were being eaten in the surface film, not on top of it. This fly is effective because the body rides below the surface, while the shell lies in the film. In this way, it imitates an emerging insect that is trapped in the surface tension—just the kind of helpless snack game fish can't seem to resist. Success increases when the shell is treated with flotant to keep it high in the film. This treatment also makes the white poly yarn easier to see. Use care not to get any flotant on the body, though, as it needs to soak up water so that it rides in the water instead of on it.

The Dräpar'n can be taken for several different varieties of emerging insects, which is useful in situations like the one described above. This smorgasbord includes mayflies, sedges, midges, and stoneflies. (The Swedish stoneflies are size 16 and 18.) By keeping the body slim the fly imitates a mayfly emerger. Adding some additional bulk to the body makes it look like a sedge or caddis.

The Dräpar'n works especially well on trout and grayling, but it has also proven effective for char. Dennis reports that most of his clients laugh when they first see the fly. But once they've had a chance to see how effective it is, they can't wait to try it. Like most other guide flies, this one is a quick tie and has proved its worth on the water.

## Tying Steps

1. Lay down a thread base to the bend of the hook.

2. Tie in a 2-inch (5cm) strip of white poly yarn, letting it hang over the bend.

3. Dub a body of black Fly-Rite the full length of the hook.

4. Fold the yarn over the top of the body, forming a top shell with the tag sticking out past the eye. Bind the yarn down.

5. Make a head.

6. Trim the yarn so that it extends a short distance past the eye.

**Materials**
Hook: TMC 5263, sizes 2–6
Thread: Yellow UTC, 7/0
Eyes: Gold Dazle-Eyes
Body: Light yellow UV Ice Dub
Rib: Fine gold Largartun wire
Wing: Cream/ginger Whiting
　　hen neck or hen back
Collar: Cream/ginger Whiting
　　hen neck or hen back
Head: Light yellow UV Ice Dub

## 52
### Collier's Vanilla Ice Matuka
*Tied by Dennis Collier*

Dennis Collier of Rocky Mountain Anglers (www.rockymtanglers.com) in Boulder, Colorado, for some time now has been experimenting with new materials to make existing patterns even more effective. This pattern is a prime example of his success.

For anglers who like Matuka streamers, this is a dynamite fly. It combines Collier's Vanilla Ice color scheme and the non-fouling virtues of the Matuka wing design. And the Dazle-Eyes add weight. Dennis claims that once you try it, you'll find a permanent spot for it in your fly box.

Fish the Vanilla Ice Matuka with a cast that quarters down and across. Be sure to add a downstream mend to put a belly in the line as the fly starts the crosscurrent swing. This mend keeps the fly broadside to the current, making it more visible to fish.

## Tying Steps

1. Lay down a thread base.

2. Tie in the eyes under the hook, slightly behind the eye.

3. Tie in the wire for ribbing.

4. Dub a body and wrap forward to just behind the eye, and then figure-eight around the eyes.

5. Measure two or three wing hackles at twice the length of the shank. Strip the bottom fibers off the hackles where the wing will touch the body. Tie them in behind the eye. Wet your fingers and stroke the wing fibers up. You can also add several strands of pearl UV IC Wing fibers to each side of the Matuka wing.

6. Rib the wire over the body and use a bodkin to separate the hackle fibers so the rib won't mash any hackle fibers down. Tie off behind the eye.

7. Wrap several turns of hen neck hackle just behind the eyes to make a collar.

8. Dub a small head and finish off.

9. Use the hook side of a piece of Velcro to rough up the entire body and head. This softens the profile and releases the UV fibers. It also adds an enticing purple halo around the fly.

**Materials**
Hook: TMC, sizes 6-10, or TMC
3761, sizes 12-16
Thread: Black, 6/0 or 8/0
Bead: Gold, sized to hook
Body and Collar: Umpqua Sparkle
Blend, dark stone
Tail: Rusty brown biots
Wing: Ginger biots
Rib: Gold wire
Legs: Black hen fibers

**53**

Hart's Dark Lord
*Tied by Ron Hart*

Every once in a while you meet a guide who turns out to be especially thoughtful. I don't mean well-mannered: I mean someone who thinks. Ron Hart of Hart's Guide Service (530-926-2431) in Mount Shasta, California, is just that kind of guide.

He began wondering why the Prince Nymph worked so well in pocket water, but not in slower waters. He also noticed that after a week of hitting the same pocket water with the Prince Nymph, it didn't produce like it had the first day. His conclusion was that the white wings weren't natural enough. Even though white made the trout curious enough to taste the fly once, they quickly realized it wasn't an organic food item.

Ron was pretty sure the contrast of the white wing over the dark body on the original fly triggered the bite. So his goal was to develop an attractive contrast, but with more natural coloration. Because the wing needed to be darker than the white Prince wing, the body had to be darker, too. As true black and stark white are not found in nature, he chose Umpqua's Dark Stone dubbing for the body. To provide the necessary contrast, Ron selected ginger biots for the wings.

This necessitated a few other changes. The tinsel rib on the Prince tended to fall apart and so it was replaced by wire. The hackle collar didn't look much like legs so he switched to soft hen fibers. Finally, he didn't like the thread showing behind the bead head, so he lightly dubbed over it.

When the fly was ready, Ron did some interesting tests to prove its effectiveness. He fished a two-fly rig composed of a #14 Prince Nymph and the Dark Lord. Eleven of the first 13 fish were caught on the new fly. In pocket water, the new fly won just 6-to-5 over the Prince, but in a slow, 6-foot-deep run every fish was taken on the new fly.

The original fly, named for *The Lord of the Rings* books, spun off a series of different colors. Ron's success also led to another good thing: he's now on the Umpqua Feather Merchant design team. It just goes to show you what can be accomplished when you find a way to break out of your old habits.

## Tying Steps

1. Slide a bead up to the hook eye.

2. Lay down a thread base and dub a ball at the bend of the hook.

3 Tie in a tail consisting of two biots split apart by the dubbing ball.

4. Tie in wire ribbing.

5. Dub a tapered body and wind forward about three-quarters of the way to the eye.

6. Wind the rib forward.

7. Tie in hen hackle fibers as legs on each side.

8. Tie in the biot wings just a bit shorter than the body length.

9. Whip finish the head.

10. Cover the head wraps with a thinly dubbed collar.

**MATERIALS**
Hook: Nymph hook, 1XL or 2XL,
    sizes 10–16
Thread: Black, 6/0
Eyes: Small lead dumbbell
Tail and Body: Pheasant tail fibers,
    dyed or natural
Legs/Gills: Ostrich herl

## 54

**PHEASANT TAIL
DUMBBELL**
*Tied by Jim Krul*

I stopped by my old friend Jim Krul's place the other day (www.flyfishingu.net); as usual, he was at his vise, which is where he makes his living. I was determined to ignore his past poor treatment of me, so I politely asked, "What's that you're tying?"

He replied, "It's a Pheasant Tail, Dumbbell."

"No need to get nasty," I said.

"No," he explained, "it's a Pheasant Tail Nymph tied with tiny dumbbell eyes."

I had to admit it looked cute, but it's what the fish think that's important.

Why use dumbbell eyes rather than a bead? Jim claims the extra weight makes it move like a miniature Clouser Minnow. The up-and-down motion created by the heavy eyes make the nymph look like a natural nymph swimming in the water.

I noticed that the pheasant tail fibers were an unusual color. "What's that?" I asked.

"Pheasant, dyed," he said.

"I know the pheasant died," I told him. "But what is it?"

As it turned out, he had pheasant tails dyed in about 10 colors. If you want to try some dyed pheasant tails or tiny dumbbells, get in touch with Jim at 845-855-5182 to request a copy of his catalog. Just don't ask too many questions; you'll feel better that way.

## TYING STEPS

1. Build a thread base along the hook shank.

2. Use figure-eight wraps to tie in a pair of small dumbbell eyes back from the eye, leaving room for a head.

3. Advance the thread to the bend and tie in a bunch of pheasant tail fibers as a tail. The tail should be about as long as the hook shank. The number of fibers is determined by the size of the hook: the larger the size, the greater the number of fibers.

4. Make a body by wrapping the fibers up to the eyes and tie in behind them. Leave the fibers untrimmed.

5. Make some legs/gills of ostrich herl by wrapping behind and in front of the dumbbell.

6. Pull the pheasant fibers over the top of both the ostrich herl and the dumbbell and tie off.

7. Make a head and whip finish. You can also leave some fibers sticking out to look like legs, but I doubt the fish really care.

MATERIALS
Hook: Tiemco 2457, sizes 12–16
Bead: Copper, ⅛ for size 12, ³⁄₃₂ for size 14 and 16
Thread: Black, 6/0 or 8/0
Abdomen: Mottled dark turkey tail fibers
Rib: Fine copper wire
Thorax: Black Ice Dubbing

55

Turkey Bead Head
*Tied by Ralph Wood*

Ralph Wood from the C&R Guide Service (www.wildtrout.com) in Grass Valley, California, sent this pattern along. He notes that it was invented by Northern California fly-fishing guide Dave Foster. Ralph does some commercial tying during the winter, and he gets bored tying the same pattern over and over. When Ice Dubbing first came out, he began experimenting. As it turned out, this modified pattern is now Ralph's go-to trout fly on the North Fork Yuba River. It has also proven effective on the Truckee, Feather, Upper Sacramento, and Pitt Rivers, and Ralph has even used it to take steelhead from the Lower Yuba.

Ralph says the fly looks like mayfly and caddis nymphs. He likes to fish it in deep runs and riffles as the tail fly on a double-nymph rig. He also uses it as a dropper below a dry fly in shallower water. His favorite time to run it as a dropper—below a dry October Caddis Stimulator—is in the fall, just before the fish begin migrating to deeper water as the temperature drops.

If you can't find the turkey tail fibers through your normal fly-tying supplier, consider swapping a dozen of these flies for feathers from a turkey hunter in your area.

## Tying Steps

1. Slide a copper bead up to the hook eye.

2. Lay down a smooth thread base to the center of the hook bend.

3. Cut three or four turkey tail fibers for tails and attach them with two wraps of thread. The tails should be ¼ to ⅓ inch long.

4. Tie in a length of fine copper wire.

5. Cover the thread base with a light coat of Flexament.

6. Wrap the turkey fibers two-thirds of the way to the eye and tie off.

7. Reverse wrap the copper wire four or five turns to the end of the body and tie off.

8. Dub Ice Dubbing into a full thorax behind the bead.

9. Whip finish and pick out a little of the Ice Dubbing to give it extra flash.

## MATERIALS

Hook: Any pupa or emerger hook, sizes 14–18
Thread: Black, 8/0
Body: Rust/brown Antron dubbing
Underwing: Gray Antron
Overwing: Dark dun CDC
Thorax: Olive Antron dubbing
Hackle: Olive-dyed grizzly, clipped on the bottom

## 56

### DIPPING CADDIS
*Tied by Ken Tutalo*

K en and Michele Tutalo run the Baxter House B&B and River Outfitters in Roscoe, New York (www.baxterhouse.net). Their fly shop features many patterns developed by Ken and his guides specifically for hatches on the Willowemoc, Beaverkill, and Delaware Rivers.

The egg-laying caddis flights of the upper Delaware River can be extremely heavy. So much so that it's often difficult to get the fish to pay attention to your fly. These caddis are often referred to as "dippers" due to the manner in which the flies return to the surface time after time to deposit all their eggs. Ken needed a fly that would be seen by the fish even when thousands of naturals were present.

The technique for fishing this pattern also contributes to its ability to be noticed by trout. Ken likes to give some action to the fly in both fast and slow water. Because the abdomen hangs down below the surface, twitching the fly pushes the body through the water, causing enough disturbance to fool the fish into seeing the fly as a natural that's actively depositing its eggs (or ovipositing for you sticklers).

Ken also reports that this pattern works well during any stage of caddis activity; it even holds its own as a non-hatch searching pattern. The Dipping Caddis should be considered more of a style of tying than a specific imitation, and the color and size can be changed to match caddis on your home waters. Ken proved this last summer on several Montana rivers, where the fly brought many fish to the net.

## Tying Steps

1. Tie in halfway down the bend of the hook.

2. Dub a tapered body, starting halfway down the bend and ending half the distance to the hook point.

3. Tie in a small underwing of gray Antron.

4. Tie in several dun colored CDC feathers to create a caddis-shaped wing.

5. Tie in a slightly oversized hackle by the tip for palmering.

6. Dub a thorax forward to just behind the eye. When done correctly, the wing will look like it is sticking directly out of the thorax and will be in line with it.

7. Wind the hackle forward over the thorax to behind the eye. Tie off.

8. Clip the hackle from the underside of the fly.

**MATERIALS**
Hook: TMC 100, sizes 10–16
Thread: Black, 6/0
Body: Black 2mm foam
Underbody (optional): Black UV dubbing
Wing: Elk hair
Legs: Black rubber
Indicator: Yellow or white foam

**57**

MILLER'S MUTATION
*Tied by Chris Conway*

C hris Conway runs Wild Basin Outfitters, Ltd. (www.wildbasinoutfitters.com) near Rocky Mountain National Park in Colorado. He reports that the Mutation was developed by guide J. D. Miller. After studying insects on his home waters throughout the summer, Miller designed this fly to imitate any one of several naturals.

Versatility is the greatest thing about this pattern. Fish it dead drift along the foam lines and it will pull big fish out of hiding. Tied in black, tan, orange, or cinnamon, it looks like a caddis or small stonefly.

J. D. typically has clients cast this pattern to rising trout. If it's refused, he'll trim some of the elk hair and separate it into two wings. This gives it the look of a flying ant. Cut the wing off completely and you have a creditable beetle imitation. Carry 10 Mutations in various colors and you can imitate at least four different primary food sources in Rocky Mountain National Park. How's that for getting your money's worth?

Chris likes to fish this pattern on the Big Thompson River, which starts as a roily mountain stream in the Park. By the time the river reaches the Moraine Park area, it slows and winds its way through a grassy meadow. Undercut banks in this area harbor some sizeable browns. Chris casts the Miller's Mutation up to the head of a pool and gives it a quick mend to keep enough slack in the line for a drag-free drift through the deeper bends. When a fish takes, he gently tightens the line until he feels pressure, and then sets the hook.

If you're an angler who doesn't like to carry dozens of different patterns for every possible situation, the Miller's Mutation may be just the ticket.

## Tying Steps

1. Cut the foam to shape and size it to the hook.

2. Lay down a thread base that ends at a spot above the barb.

3. Tie in the foam body facing away from the eye.

4. Dub a body with black UV to just behind the eye (this step is optional). Then move the thread back about one-quarter of the shank length.

5. Fold the foam body back over the shank and tie down to make a head shape.

6. At this same point, tie in elk hair on top so the tips extend just past the back of the body.

7. Also at this same point, tie in rubber legs. Trim them to equal lengths.

8. Finally, yet again at this same point, tie in a small foam indicator.

9. Whip finish and cement the threads.

**58**

Electric Leech
*Tied by J. D. Miller*

MATERIALS

Hook: TMC 200R, sizes 8–12
Thread: Black, 6/0
Bead: Standard, ⅛ to ⁵⁄₃₂ depending on
  hook size
Underbody (optional): Lead wire
Wing: Wapsi Black Pine Squirrel
  Zonker strip (or brown or olive)
Body: Wapsi Rainbow Sparkle Braid
Collar: Montana Fly Company Henry's
  Fork Hackle, black

J. D. Miller of Kinsley Outfitters (www.kinsleyoutfitters.com) in Boulder, Colorado, created the Electric Leech because he wanted a pattern with the sleek profile of a real leech, yet with lots of movement and just the right amount of flash to get the attention of large trout. He uses the Electric Leech on the lakes in and around Rocky Mountain National Park and on the private waters of Sylvan Dale Ranch. It's produced trout over 20 inches on Spinney Mountain Reservoir, Eleven Mile Reservoir, and the Delaney Butte Lakes in Colorado and in Hebgen Lake, Clark Canyon Reservoir, and Georgetown Lake in Montana—all some of the toughest trophy stillwaters in the Rockies. In fact, this fly has accounted for more large fish than anything else in J. D.'s fly box.

He prefers to walk the lake banks looking for cruising fish. When he spots one, he'll cast the fly 5 to 7 feet ahead and start retrieving with slow, steady strips. Once he has the fish's attention, he strips faster to imitate a fleeing baitfish. Most of J. D.'s hookups are solid strikes, where the fish just inhales the Electric Leech. The fly can also be fished dead drift in rivers where leeches are present.

Not surprisingly, the Electric Leech has accounted for bass, walleye, and the odd pike, too. It should work wonders for you in any water where leeches show up regularly.

## Tying Steps

1. Place a bead on the hook and lay down a thread base to the bend.

2. Cut a Zonker strip about one and a half to two times the hook length and tie it in at the bend.

3. Fold the strip back toward the tail and build up a small thread dam. This will keep it from sliding toward the eye after you pull it forward to cover the body.

4. Tie in rainbow braid and wrap forward to the bead, making a body.

5. Unfold the Zonker strip, laying it over the body and tie in at the eye.

6. Tie in a hackle and take two or three turns to make a collar. Tie off.

7. Stroke the collar fibers back, and then take a couple of turns of thread to even up the fibers.

8. Whip finish and cement.

**59**

OlIGOCHAETE
WORM
*Tied by Fox Statler*

MATERIAlS
Hook: Daiichi Bent Shank 2170 series, sizes
12–14
Thread: Red or fluorescent red, 8/0
Weight (optional): Lead wire, .035
Body: Small to medium Ultra Chenille in
fluorescent shell pink, fluorescent pink,
fluorescent red, shrimp pink, or wine
Marker: Red Prismacolor pen or red
permanent marker

Fox Statler (www.fishinwhattheysee.com) is from Salem, Arkansas, where he's been guiding for 20 years on the White River and North Fork White River. The development of his Oligochaete Worm is a most unusual story that combines some keen observation with the Discovery Channel and the Internet. (By the way, it's pronounced "ol-i-go-ket.")

It all started when he noticed some trout moving up to feed in the tracks he made in 18 inches of water, where he had dislodged a thick crust of dead olive-brown algae. Closer inspection turned up a pink aquatic worm. Once in hand, the worm crawled just like an earthworm. When released, however, it coiled up like a corkscrew with just a short tail sticking out. After it hit the bottom, it uncoiled and crawled away. The next 50 worms he captured did the same thing. Fox knew he was onto something.

An Internet search informed Fox that there are more than a hundred types of aquatic worms, known as Oligochaete. Some even have eyes. They're typically 3 to 4 inches long and ⅛ inch in diameter. The colors range from shell pink to cerise on the main body, and they have bright red ends due to the concentration of blood vessels close to the skin. Based on this research, Fox now ties all his Oligochaete Worms with red ends, regardless of the main body color.

On the Discovery Channel, Fox learned that the worms curl up in moving water until they're able to uncoil and crawl away to hide in mud or gravel—just like the ones he had observed first-hand. Who says you can't learn anything from TV?

Fox notes that it's easy to add weight to this pattern because of the coiled shape. For shallow conditions, he goes without weight, but he adds up to 10 wraps of lead wire for fishing faster water.

## TYING STEPS

1. Lay down a thread base.

2. Wrap up to 10 turns of lead wire at the middle of the shank.

3. Wrap thread over the wire, finishing with the thread at the eye.

4. Apply some cement to the thread wrappings.

5. Cut a 3- to 4-inch piece of Ultra Chenille. Color the last ¼ inch of each end with a red pen.

6. Tie in the chenille at the bend, leaving a ¼-inch tail.

7. Lay a narrow knitting needle or large toothpick on the shank and wind the chenille over to form loose loops. The still-wet cement will bind the wraps to the bottom of the shank.

8. Remove the toothpick. Tie down the chenille at the eye with the red end showing but not hanging off.

9. Whip finish and cement.

**MATERIALS**

Hook: Tiemco 100, sizes 18–22
Thread: Gray, 14/0 Griffiths
Bead: Gunmetal midge glass bead, Killer Caddis
Wing: Krystal Flash
Tail: Light or dark dun hackle fibers
Body: Gray fine dubbing
Rib: Silver extra-fine Largartun wire

## 60

GUNMETAL SPARKLE
WING RS2
*Tied by Chris Eisenhard*

Chris Eisenhard of Colorado Fly Fishing Adventures (www.coloradoflyfishing-adventures.com) likes to cook up something new by combining the effective characteristics of existing flies into new creations. The basis for this pattern is the RS2. A few local tiers in his area started tying the sparkle wing RS2 several years ago. He took it a step further, adding the gunmetal bead and the wire wrap for a segmented body, both of which he'd had success with on previous patterns.

His intuition was correct, and the Gunmetal Sparkle Wing RS2 has produced "a ton" of fish for him and his clients. So far, it has accounted for rainbows, brookies, browns, cutthroats, and whitefish. Chris thinks this pattern works well because it resembles an emerging mayfly. The Krystal Flash wing is a realistic imitation of an emerging natural, and the rib and bead get the fish's attention.

The fly works particularly well on tailwaters and freestone rivers. It can be fished by itself in the surface film or as the dropper on a double-nymph rig. It produces fish year-round, but is especially effective during the early stages of a Blue-Winged Olive hatch.

## TYING STEPS

1. Slide a glass bead onto the hook.

2. Lay down a thread base to the bend and return the thread two-thirds of the way back to the bead.

3. Tie in wings by looping two strands of Krystal Flash.

4. Tie in a tail of light or dark dun hackle fibers.

5. Tie in a length of extra-fine silver Largartun wire at the tail to be used for ribbing.

6. Dub a tapered body of fine gray dubbing up to behind the wing.

7. Wrap the wire ribbing to behind the wing.

8. Apply more dubbing and continue the body to the bead.

9. Whip finish and cement.

**MATERIALS**
Hook: Daiichi 1120 or TMC 2457, sizes 14–16
Thread: Black, 8/0
Body: Diamondbraid or Antron yarn
Wing: White poly or Antron yarn

**61**

SPARKLE R.A.M.
CADDIS
*Tied by John Hildenbrand*

This pattern includes just two materials. Now that's quick and easy!

John Hildenbrand is from Pawling, New York, and he guides around the Croton watershed and Housatonic and Farmington Rivers for The Angler's Den (www.anglers-den.com). In addition to the fly shop, this is also the new home of English Angling Trappings, a huge catalog of tying materials. Contact them for a copy.

This pattern was shown to John about 10 years ago by a guide in West Yellowstone, Montana. It's basically a R.A.M. Caddis, developed by Ross Merigold, with variations of the original materials and color. The Sparkle R.A.M. Caddis is John's go-to subsurface fly 90 percent of the time. He usually fishes it as a dropper behind a bead head, although when conditions are right he'll occasionally use it as an emerger under a dry fly. He has such confidence in this pattern that he doesn't even mind fishing pools other fishermen have pounded.

The color and flash serve as attractors, while the profile can be quite realistic. This fly works well for all types of trout in clear or dirty water.

Speed is critical when tying commercially, and John can tie about four-dozen of this pattern per hour. He doesn't bother wrapping a thread base over the entire hook shank prior to wrapping the body, and he doesn't use head cement. "I don't care if I lose lots of these on a trip. If it gets caught on something, just break it off quickly and put another on," he says.

This is the ultimate in simple flies, and John's clients are often surprised with the results it produces. Keep several colors in your fly box and fish them with confidence.

## Tying Steps

1. Tie in a piece of diamondbraid just behind the hook eye.

2. Bring the thread to the rear of the hook as you continue to wrap over the diamondbraid, forming a smooth underbody.

3. Bring the thread forward, ending close to the hook eye.

4. Wrap the diamondbraid from the rear of the hook forward to the eye. Twist the heck out of it so you can form a neat, segmented body. Butt the wraps of body material up against each other as you wrap forward, leaving no gaps.

5. Secure the diamondbraid and trim the excess.

6. Tie in a piece of Antron or poly yarn that slants backward to simulate an emergent wing. Trim to size and shape.

7. Whip finish.

# SALT WATER

**MATERIALS**
Hook: Mustad 34007, size 4
Thread: Danville fluorescent orange, flat-waxed
Eyes: Small gold or black bead chain
Weed Guard: 17- or 20-pound Mason monofilament
Tail: Rabbit fur strip
Body: Orange pearl Ice Chenille

62

DUMB DRUM
*Tied by Barry Hoffman*

"Redfish aren't the brightest fish in the pond," according to Captain Barry Hoffman (www.flatsguide.com). Barry guides for bonefish, tarpon, and redfish around Islamorada, Biscayne Bay, and Florida Bay. He wanted a simple fly that ties up in just a couple of minutes and that also worked well in the Keys. The Dumb Drum is what he developed. The fly is not only a hot one for redfish; Barry also uses it for snook and seatrout.

The materials Barry chose have important influences on how this fly behaves. The fly needed to be effective in very shallow, murky water, often as thin as 8 inches. It also had to be able to suspend in the water column long enough to give the fish a good chance to see it before it sank into the turtle grass.

The rabbit fur imparts plenty of action, even when the fly is fished slowly. And the Ice Chenille adds a bit of flash and traps some air, giving the fly a slow descent. This latter characteristic is the most important, because the sighting distance is short in murky water.

Due to the normally muddy conditions, short, slow twitches 6 to 8 inches ahead of the path of the fish is all it should take to encourage a strike. The small size and profile of the Dumb Drum make for accurate casting even under windy conditions.

## TYING STEPS

1. Lay down a thread base from the eye to a point just above the barb of the hook.

2. Tie in a 4-inch piece of Mason monofilament. Start behind the eye and tie the mono along the hook shank to a spot above the hook point. Leave the mono sticking out past the bend. It will be looped back later to complete the weed guard.

3. Attach bead-chain eyes a bit behind the hook eye, leaving room to tie off the mono weed guard.

4. Tie in a short piece of rabbit fur strip as a tail, just ahead of the hook bend.

5. Tie in Ice Chenille behind the bead-chain eyes. Wrap down to the tail and back, creating a plump body. Tie off forward of the eyes.

6. Loop the weed guard forward, under the hook, and tie in ahead of the eyes. Leave enough of a loop below to protect the hook point.

7. Cement the head.

## MATERIALS

Hook: Varivas 990S, size 1
Thread: Fine monocord
Eyes: Spirit River ³⁄₁₆ dumbbell eyes
    and #2 silver prism stick-on eyes
Body: Bill's Bodi-Braid, pearl
Overwing: Light tan/olive bucktail
Underwing: White bucktail
Flash: Pearl Flashabou

# 63

## CAPE COD
## CLOUSER
*Tied by Jim Ellis*

C aptain Jim Ellis of the Haystaddle Hill Guide Service on Cape Cod, Mass-achusetts (www.charternet.com/flyfish/haystaddle), sent along his go-to fly for striped bass in the spring and early summer. He uses it on the sand flats, especially where sand eels are the predominant forage fish for stripers.

Jim credits his friend Peter Alves with adapting a standard Clouser pattern to include the Gotcha-style. Peter noticed this tying technique on bonefish flies used in the Bahamas. He also noticed that this style resulted in foul-proof flies and thought this would be an advantage for striper flies back home.

Capt. Ellis says the Cape Cod Clouser is best fished on a clear, intermediate line in 1 to 10 feet of water. Almost any color combination is possible, but light tans, light olives, and yellows seem to product best. At times, even an all-white version can be a good bet. He fishes it just like you would any other Clouser, by experimenting with different stripping speeds and pauses until the fish let him know he's nailed it.

## TYING STEPS

1. Tie on dumbbell eyes, being sure to leave room between the dumbbell and the hook eye for tying in additional materials and to form a head.

2. Tie in a length of Bill's Bodi-Braid and make a body by wrapping down well into the bend and back to a point in front of the eyes.

3. In front of the dumbbell eyes, tie in a small bunch of white bucktail below the hook, making sure it extends about 3 inches beyond the bend of the hook. (The dumbbell eyes will cause the fly to swim upside down so the white bucktail will actually be the belly of the fly.)

4. Tie in 4 to 10 strands of pearl Flashabou at the post where the white bucktail was tied in. These should extend a little farther than the white bucktail and the ends should be cut to different lengths.

5. Tie in a small bunch of tan/olive bucktail, also in front of the eyes and the same length as the white bucktail.

6. Press on the prism eyes.

7. Make a head in front of the eyes and whip finish the thread wraps.

8. Epoxy the thread wraps and run it behind the eyes Gotcha-style. This keeps the wing materials close against the body and prevents tangling.

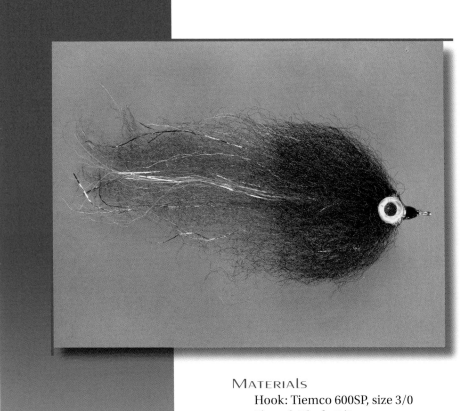

## Materials

Hook: Tiemco 600SP, size 3/0
Thread: Black, 3/0
Eyes: 3-D molded, 6.0 silver or pearl
Lateral Line: Blue Flashabou
Wing: Purple Kinky Fiber blended with
pearl Flashabou
Collar: Black Kinky Fiber
Head: Epoxy over black thread

## 64

### Purple
### Kinky Death
*Tied by Lou Fitzner*

The name of this fly sounds like a cross between a Sherlock Holmes novel and an adult movie, but Capt. Lou Fitzner (fitnzner@attglobal.net), who guides out of Connecticut and New York, insists his fly is rated "G" (for great?). It's a variation of the standard Purple Death, but this fly is more durable than the original, whose wing of rooster hackle didn't always hold up well.

Capt. Lou says the standard overall length is 5½ inches, and there's a longer version at a whopping 7½ inches. In spite of its mouth-filling size, it's a delight to cast. The reason for this it that the Kinky Fiber doesn't absorb water, which means that it remains light even when wet. Good thing, too, because swinging a 7½-inch fly with any weight to it is like tossing a house cat through the air.

There's something universally appealing about the Purple Kinky Death's profile and translucence. It works from New England—for striped bass—right down through Florida for tarpon. In addition, Lou's clients have used it to take bluefish.

## Tying Steps

1. Lay down a thread base from the eye to the middle of the shank.

2. Make a lateral line by tying in a few strands of blue Flashabou.

3. Tie in equal lengths of purple Kinky Fiber above and below the hook shank. The first course should be about 5 inches long. Each new course should be tied in a little closer to the eye and should be shorter than the last by ½ inch, which creates a tapered profile.

4. Repeat for a total of four courses, ending ¼ inch behind the eye.

5. Create a collar by tying in small bunches of black Kinky Fiber all around the hook shank.

6. Glue on 3-D molded eyes about ½ inch behind the hook eye.

7. Trim the fibers, make a head, and whip finish.

8. Coat the exposed thread, the eyes, and a little bit of the fibers between the eyes with 5-minute epoxy. Applying the epoxy to the fibers keeps them in place and prevents them from fouling or twisting around the hook shank.

MATERIALS
Hook: Umpqua, pre-bent for
    backbends, size 2
Thread: Fluorescent orange, pink,
    or Kelly green Gudebrod, 3/0
Body: Estaz in fluorescent orange,
    pink, or Kelly green
Eyes: Bead chain
Wing: Polar bear hair

65

BEAR BONES
*Tied by Dave Sutton*

This fly comes compliments of Dave Sutton. If you're thinking, "I know that name." You're right. He's guided for ESPN's *Addictive Fishing*. Capt. Dave runs Backcountry Charters (www.saltwater-flyfisherman.com) out of Redlands, Florida, where he guides over two hundred days each year. He's kept this fly under wraps for several years, but has now decided to share the wealth. Lucky for us, too, as his clients refer to the Bear Bones as the "magic bait."

This fly takes its name from the polar bear wing. It's worth the trouble to find polar bear hair because of its light-refracting ability. Dave says bucktail is not quite as good, although it does provide more flotation.

He controls the fishing depth by selecting bead-chain eyes in various sizes: heavy for deep water, light for medium depths, and no eyes for shallow water. Regardless of the depth, he fishes this fly on a 10- to 12-foot leader with a full floating line. With each pull of the retrieve, the fly is lifted off the bottom—just like a shrimp moves. The backbend hook allows you to fish in heavy grass or over fan coral bottom without hangups.

Dave's 12 years of experience around Biscayne Bay and Everglades National Park have taught him the importance of color selection. The pink and green work best for bonefish, while the orange does well on redfish. The green can also be used for snook and seatrout.

## TYING STEPS

1. Tie in a thread base.

2. Add bead-chain eyes to the top of the hook shank. Wrap heavily, and then wrap thread base to the bend of the hook. Cement all thread wraps.

3. Tie in Estaz and wrap over before the cement dries. This will make a very durable fly.

4. Wrap the Estaz back to the bend and forward again to create a bulky body. Be sure to wrap the Estaz around and in front of the eyes.

5. Cement thread wraps.

6. Tie in a wing of polar bear ahead of the eyes and cement all wraps.

7. Coat head with high-gloss cement.

## MATERIALS

Hook: Tiemco 800S, sizes 2–6
Thread: Uni-mono, fine
Eyes: Spirit River Tape Eyes, size 2.0
Body: Bill's Bodi-Braid, silver
Underbody: Gliss N' Glow, MOP and
    Clear Ice
Overbody: Flouro-Fibre, olive and gray;
    Gliss N' Glow, MOP root beer
Cement: Devcon 2-Ton Epoxy

## 66

### SAND LANCE
*Tied by Chris West*

This fly was designed by Chris West (www.pugetsoundflyfishing.com), who also guides for Emerald Water Anglers (www.emeraldwateranglers.com) in Seattle, Washington. Chris notes that the sand lance is the most abundant baitfish in the Northwest. Given that they are also common along the East Coast, the pattern is surely worth a try there, as well.

The Sand Lance has become Chris's favorite saltwater searching pattern around kelp beds, rock ledges, eelgrass, and sandy-bottomed areas where the baitfish thrive. It serves the same purpose as the Beadhead Pheasant Tail often does in fresh water. It also turned out to be a good pattern for use when bait balls aren't present to help concentrate fishing action. Be sure to retrieve the fly with long strips.

So what species have been taken on the Sand Lance? How about sea-run cutthroat, steelhead, and coho, chinook, pink, and chum salmon. That's quite a track record.

## Tying Steps

1. Tie in Bodi-Braid behind the eye, and wrap to the bend.

2. Wrap thread from the eye to the bend and back.

3. Wrap the Bodi-Braid back to ¼ inch from the eye.

4. Measure and cut the materials for steps 5–9 to 3-inch lengths before tying in.

5. Tie in three to six strands of MOP Gliss N' Glow under the hook at the ¼-inch mark so they're pointing toward the eye and away from the bend (backward).

6. Tie in 18 strands of olive Flouro-Fibre on top of the hook, pointing toward the eye.

7. Tie in 25 strands of Clear Ice Gliss N' Glow, backward, on the bottom side of the hook.

8. Tie in 25 strands of gray Flouro-Fibre, backward, on the top of the hook.

9. Repeat the first step with four strands of Gliss N' Glow MOP root beer.

10. Pull the top wings back over the hook and secure with thread at the tie-in spot.

11. Pull the bottom wings back under the hook and tie in.

12. Whip finish.

13. Apply eyes.

14. Epoxy over both eyes, completely covering the head.

15. Place in a turner for an hour and then let the epoxy cure for 24 hours.

**MATERIALS**
Hook: Eagle Claw 413, sizes 1/0–4/0
Thread: Monofilament
Weight: Lead wire, .019
Underbody: White hackle flanked by
   White Super Hair
Wing: Chartreuse Super Hair
Flash: Pearl saltwater Flashabou
Eyes: Molded silver eyes

**67**

BAJA DEEP DIVER
*Tied by Gary Graham*

Some of the guides who have shared their patterns here have held world records. I, myself, hold the record for most fall-ins in a single season. Then there's Gary and Yvonne Graham, who run Baja On The Fly (www.bajafly.com). Gary has held two world records for bigeye tuna and halibut. The following year he broke another two records for these same species using lighter lines. Yvonne was the first woman in 25 years to catch a marlin on 12-pound test, and she's also held several other world records. Gary has been named one of the top ten anglers in the United States, and he has won several California light-tackle billfish tournaments. He's even caught a world record from his front yard. So when Gary sent this pattern along, I made sure to pay attention.

This fly was designed to have swimming characteristics similar to a Clouser, but without the addition of dumbbell eyes, which are harder to cast. Gary and Yvonne fish the Baja Deep Diver with a shooting head or an intermediate sinking line. It's designed to get deep in the water column. Following the cast, let the fly sink, varying the countdown until the fish are located. Begin the retrieve with several long, abrupt pulls, and then let it flutter back down a few feet. Repeat the process.

When fish are crashing bait on the surface, let the fly sink and retrieve it as slowly as possible so it looks like an injured baitfish. If you're fishing offshore, use a two-handed retrieve, moving the fly as quickly as possible.

The Baja Deep Diver has proven effective on dorado, yellowfin tuna, African pompano, gaffsail pompano, jack crevalle, cabrilla, ladyfish, snook, halibut, pargo, palometa amarillo, needlefish, and sierra. The first time Gary tried this fly he caught an 18-pound palometa amarilla, the first of this species ever caught on a fly in Baja.

## Tying Steps

1. Take 25 wraps of .019 lead wire around the shank near the eye.

2. Tie in one white hackle on each side of the hook.

3. Turn the hook over and tie in white Super Hair. It should extend one hook length beyond the bend.

4. Tie in chartreuse Super Hair, extending two shank lengths beyond the bend.

5. Turn the hook over and tie in a belly of pearl saltwater Flashabou. It should be as long as the chartreuse Super Hair. (This fly rides hook point up in the water.)

6. Attach ¼-inch molded silver eyes.

7. Finish with 5-minute Z-Poxy.

## Materials

Hook: Owner "Flyliner" Cutting Point,
size 2/0
Thread: Yellow "G" Gudebrod
Tail: Electric yellow Polar Fibre Hair,
topped by white, topped by hot pink
Flash: Fishent silver Gliss N' Glow
Body: Kelly green Ice Chenille, large
Head: Brass cone head

68

CONEHEAD Nicky
*Tied by Doug Sinclair*

The name for this fly sounds like an insult, but it's actually a speckled trout and redfish pattern from Capt. Doug Sinclair of the Fly Fishing Academy in Grantsboro, North Carolina (www.flyfishacademy.net).

One of his clients, Nicky, asked why they don't make flies to copy the color patterns of MirrOlures. Doug's initial reply was just an explanation that certain conventions are used to design flies. But the question was enough to start Doug thinking, and he soon began devising color schemes to imitate popular lures.

This pattern was adapted from the Texas Chicken lure. Don't ask me what that is because I don't have a clue, although it's safe to assume it's a highly effective lure for light-tackle anglers. Doug ties the fly in two versions: as a floater with no weight and in the conehead version shown here.

Doug first fished this fly in an inshore estuary area called the Haystacks near Beaufort, North Carolina. It's a large grass flat that is subject to tidal fluctuations. The fly produced extremely well on a falling tide, when the big reds and seatrout were feeding on the flow of bait across the flats. It also works very well in tannic-colored water or when you need to fish in water up to 10 feet deep.

This particular pattern has a lot to offer. Doug says you can let it sink slowly, fish it like a jerk worm, or swim it like a baitfish. The motion of the fly, in combination with the materials that keep it somewhat submerged, makes it successful. Doug believes the hot pink, electric yellow, and white color combination is a natural attractor. The Polar Fibre has so strong a luminance that only a little flash is required. Also, the Gliss N' Glow is very effective, creating the impression of a real baitfish more realistically than other flash materials.

## TYING STEPS

1. Crimp or cut the barb and slide a cone onto the hook next to the eye.

2. Just above where the barb was, make six wraps of thread and tie in yellow or chartreuse Polar Fibre Hair.

3. Tie in six strands of silver Gliss N' Glow.

4. Tie in white Polar Fibre Hair.

5. Tie in hot pink Polar Fibre Hair.

6. Tie in a 6-inch length of Kelly green large Ice Chenille.

7. Wrap forward in a tight body up to the cone head.

8. Make three wraps of thread and whip finish.

9. Add a single drop of head cement at the cut point.

## MATERIALS

Hook: Mustad 34007, stainless
steel, size 4
Thread: Tan flat-waxed nylon
Eyes: Black brass bead chain
Weight: Lead wire, 0.6 mm
Feelers: Gold Krystal Flash
Body: Tan Sparkle Crab Yarn
Mouth Parts: Tan deer hair tips
Legs and Stand: 12-pound mono

**69**

ANDY'S STANDING
CRAB YARN SHRIMP
*Tied by Andy Thomsen*

ndy Thomsen (www.andysfishing.com.au) of North Queensland, Australia, guides flyfishers chasing tarpon, permit, giant travelley, snook, and barramundi, among other species. He needed a simple shrimp pattern that worked well in shallow water, and this fly was his answer. Most shrimp patterns are just too time consuming to tie. In addition to fast, easy tying, the big bonus with this fly is that it will right itself in only inches of water. The fish scarf it up.

Like most anglers here in the U.S., I didn't know much about barramundi, so I did some research. I learned they can reach 6 feet in length and weigh a whopping 130 pounds. They're found from the Persian Gulf to southern China and, of course, along the northern coast of Australia.

They all start out as males, but after maturity, at age five, they all switch to females. (I swear I'm not making this up.) Barramundi eggs hatch out in 15 to 20 *hours* and become larvae. By day five the egg yolk is completely absorbed and they are fully developed. Barramundi are known for their spectacular leaps and are considered to be one of the finest-tasting fish for the table. No wonder they're so popular.

As Andy's fly has proven so effective on game fish that eat shrimp Down Under, there's no reason to believe it won't be just as productive in any shallow water where shrimp are on the menu.

## TYING STEPS

1. Lay down a thread base the entire length of the shank.

2. Hold lead wire on the underside of the hook and tie it in from the midpoint of the shank to the hook eye.

3. Make 10 turns of lead back toward the hook eye. Cut off and tie down securely.

4. Return the thread to the bend and tie in two lengths of Krystal Flash.

5. Tie in a small bunch of stacked deer hair tips.

6. Tie eyes in on top of the deer hair using a figure-eight motion. Position the eyes to ride high.

7. Position the mono legs behind the eyes. They should be level with the hook point. Trim the excess.

8. Tie in the yarn behind the eyes and wrap toward the hook eye.

9. Tie off and cement.

10. Trim the yarn, splay out to make a tail, and trim to ¼ inch long.

**Materials**
Hook: Mustad C71S SS Circle Streamer, sizes
   1/0–3/0
Thread: Chartreuse "G" Gudebrod
Tail: Chartreuse marabou, yellow grizzly
   marabou, chartreuse Deceiver hackle, and
   gold hologram flash
Body: Chartreuse deer hair
Head: Red deer hair
Eyes: 6mm plastic eyes, yellow with black pupil
Cement: Gudebrod jig and fly head cement

## 70

### Red-Headed Mullet
*Tied by Doug Sinclair*

D oug Sinclair, of the Saltwater Fly Fishing Academy in Grantsboro, North Carolina (www.flyfishacademy.net), needed some new snook patterns before filming started on a television segment with Flip Pallet some years ago. He began tying samples in several color combinations, including green and white, yellow and white, white and red, tan and red, tan and blue, and chartreuse and red. After all the testing was finished, the chartreuse-red combination was the hands-down winner.

What's so special about this fly? I don't know, and neither does Doug. Taking the snook's perspective, Doug figures, "I'm a fish and I'm looking up to see a silhouette on the surface." So it's probably the shape that makes the most difference. Still, Doug reports that last year the tan patterns were the killers. But not this year: this year it's chartreuse the snook want. Who knows which color combinations will work next year? To be on the safe side, better tie a few of each.

About three years ago Doug was asked to do a story about the difference between fly fishing for redfish and stripers. As he'd never chased the latter, the first order of business was to head to Maine for the yearly migration. For the first hour, the Casco Bay stripers were tail-slapping the locally preferred flies. Doug asked to try his mullet pattern, which had proven so effective on fish in his home water, and immediately had a hookup. In the next hour, he hooked and landed 10 fish from 8 to 15 pounds. His two-day total on stripers with this fly was 53 fish. Now that's a killer pattern!

## TYING STEPS

1. Wrap a short thread base at the bend of the hook.

2 Attach one small clump of chartreuse marabou.

3. Tie in four strands of gold hologram flash.

4. Tie in one small fan-tail of grizzly marabou to each side of the shank.

5. Tie in four saddle hackles, two to a side, splayed outward.

6. Tie in a small clump of deer hair, stacked on top of the shank, leaving the butts to stand.

7. Spin a deer-hair body using pencil-thick bunches of chartreuse deer hair.

8. Switch to red deer hair for the last ¼ inch behind the eye.

9. Trim the bottom of the body flat and close.

10. Trim the rest of the deer hair to resemble a mullet.

11. Burn two holes into the deer hair using a Hotpoint.

12. Cement the eyes into the burned holes.

**MATERIALS**
Hook: Mustad 34007, size 1/0–2/0
Thread: Flat-waxed white
Tail: White bucktail, white saddle
hackle, and light green Krystal Flash
Body: Pearl craft braid over a Luck-E-
Strike rattle, extra small
Eyes: Holographic stick-on
Gills: Red acrylic paint

**71**

SNOOK RATTLE
*Tied by Jim Dussias*

Jim Dussias, owner of Oasis Angling Adventures, (www.oasis-angling.com) wanted to develop a fly for wary South Florida snook. The first time he tried this fly he was fishing near Key Largo. A jack crevalle hammered it on the second cast. Over the next two hours, Jim caught plenty of barracuda and jacks—but what about the snook? With previous test patterns, snook had been following the fly but not striking. Now they were rushing in to eat it. Jim's guess is that the difference-maker was the addition of sound. The fly already resembled a mullet, but it just needed that extra something. Bass anglers discovered the attractiveness of rattles long ago, so there was no reason to think it wouldn't work on other species. Evidently it does, as Jim reports he's also used this fly successfully on tarpon, peacock bass, and largemouth bass.

He uses a 30- to 50-pound shock tippet when fishing for snook near mangroves. He works as close to cover as possible, and with the heavy shock tippet he can rip the fly loose if it hangs up or keep hooked fish from diving back into the tangled roots. His preferred method of fishing the Snook Rattle is to cast and then pause so the fly can sink. He retrieves it with short jerks, letting the rattle do its work.

## Tying Steps

1. At the bend, make a tail by tying in a small bunch of bucktail and several white saddle hackles. These should extend three to four times the length of the hook shank.

2. Add a few strands of Krystal Flash that are slightly longer than the hackles.

3. Tie in a length of pearl craft braid at the bend of the hook.

4. Align the rattle on the underside of the shank, with the pointed end facing the bend.

5. Wrap thread to cover the entire hook shank and the rattle, binding the rattle to the hook. Be sure the rattle remains positioned below the shank.

6. Advance the thread to the eye and tie off.

7. Lay down a layer of Super Glue that covers the thread wraps and rattle.

8. Make a body by wrapping the craft braid forward, covering the rattle.

9. Paint gill plates with red acrylic paint.

10. Glue on eyes.

11. Coat the entire body with epoxy, including the eyes.

**72**

TUNA TUX
*Tied by Gary Bulla*

MATERIALS
  Hook: Owner Aki, 2–4/0
  Thread: Black, 3/0
  Lateral Line: Black Ultrahair
  Wing: Black arctic fox, craft fur, or other
    synthetic hair
  Belly: White arctic fox or Ultrahair
  Eyes: Spirit River red or pearl with black pupils
  Weight (optional): Black tungsten cone head
  Rib: Two strands of yellow or blue Krystal Flash

Yellowfin tuna—fearless, marauding marine wolf packs, right? Well, maybe not always. Sometimes, they're actually shy. When this happens it's time to try Gary Bulla's Tuna Tux.

Gary runs Fly Fishing Adventures (805-933-1366 or www.garybulla.com), and he developed this fly for occasions when the big boys are hanging out below schooling tuna working baitballs near the surface. At times like these, the larger fish get nervous and picky. They're usually satisfied with just taking the odd wounded baitfish drifting down from above. A fly with too much flash can turn these fish off.

Gary worked on the colors and a wide profile to imitate the local bait (sardines) with fishing captains in Las Arenas on the east coast of Baja, California. The resulting go-to fly was the Tuna Tux.

To get it below the smaller tuna, this fly is fished on a fast-sinking head after a long countdown. The best retrieve is slow, with long strips. Too much stop-and-go action and the fly will not appear to be a dead or damaged baitfish drifting down through the pack.

## Tying Steps

1. Slip a cone head (optional) over the hook point and advance it to the eye.

2. Tie in a rib (optional) at the bend and bring it forward to the eye.

2. Build a small lump behind the cone, binding it against the eye.

3. Tie in a small bunch of Ultrahair underwing (one and a half times the shank length), leaving space for two clumps of the overwing.

4. Tie in a small bunch of synthetic hair as an overwing.

5. Tie in a second bunch of overwing up against the cone. This second bunch gives the fly a broad silhouette.

6. Turn the hook over and add a small bunch of Ultrahair for the belly.

7. Build a large thread head (if no cone head is used) and glue on the eyes with Goop. Let dry.

8. Double coat head and eyes with epoxy.

MATERIALS
   Hook: Gamakatsu Octopus #4, stock #02108
   Thread: Black, 3/0
   Body: Rainy's large brown chenille
   Legs: Rainy's large round white rubber legs
   Cement: Griff's thick high gloss

73

SURFbUG III
*Tied by Richard Schwalm*

D
on't you just love saltwater flies? Most weigh six to the pound, are the size of a small cat, and usually require two or more people to make a cast of any distance. This one is different. Richard Schwalm of RCSports (805-492-4382) in Camarillo, California, has tinkered with this fly through three versions. He reports that he almost has it perfected now.

Richard was unsatisfied with the lack of consistent hookups while surf casting for bottom-feeding fish. Too often, the fish would bump or simply ignore the usual sand crab or orange-colored patterns. When he ran out of explanations for why the fish weren't cooperating for his clients, he began to experiment. A change of hook style seemed to do the trick. Hookups became more consistent, and his clients stopped muttering bad things about him behind his back.

He gave up on standard saltwater hooks. Now he uses a Gamakatsu Octopus hook. The design is unusual in that it has an offset bend that improves hooking ability because the point is out of alignment with the shank. He's also done some testing with the new circle hooks.

The double thickness of chenille helps the Surfbug soak up water. This increased weight gets the fly to the bottom where it belongs, right on the sand. The legs act like little Hawaiian outriggers, keeping the fly from turning over in the waves. They also keep the hook riding with the point up, increasing hookups.

## Tying Steps

1. Pinch the barb and place the hook in the vise point up.

2. Lay down a double thread base, whip finish, and cement the top and bottom of the thread base.

3. Invert hook, tie in rubber legs front and back, and then cement both sets at the tie-in point.

4. Tie in chenille behind the front legs and wrap back to the rear legs. Cement over the chenille body. (All this cementing makes a fly that will stand up to punishment.)

5. Bring the thread forward to the front legs, and then wind chenille forward, making a body of double thickness and with a fat profile.

6. Make a head, whip finish, and cement.

**Materials**
Hook: Mustad 34007, sizes 1/0–2/0
Thread: Black, flat-waxed size A
Eyes: Medium lead dumbbell eyes
Underwing: Olive bucktail
Overwing: White bucktail and pearl
Krystal Flash

## 74

### Olive and White Clouser Variant
*Tied by Charles Crue*

G uide clients never want to hear, "You should have been here yesterday." They aren't out there for the shore lunch. They want some action. Here's a large economy-sized fly that Capt. Charles Crue of Channel Edge Charters out of West Newbury, Massachusetts (www.channeledgecharters.com), relies on when he absolutely has to produce fish.

The Clouser Minnow has been around for quite some time, and it's been used successfully on a wide variety of fish. But Capt. Crue wanted a slimmer profile to match sand eels and silverside minnows, two natural baits that are favored by striped bass in the Merrimack River estuary where he often guides. He developed this effective adaptation simply by reducing the amount of materials and matching the colors to a new pair of naturals. Like other Clousers, this variation swims with the eyes down and hook point up.

Charles prefers to fish the Clouser Variant with a 9-weight rod and a fast-sinking, 300- to 350-grain line. He counts down to the depth he wants and then retrieves with short, fast strips. Often, the stripping is interrupted by large hungry fish like striped bass, bluefish, or even shad.

## TYING STEPS

1. Lay down a short thread base halfway to the bend.

2. Attach the dumbbell eyes on top of the shank, leaving room in front to tie in materials.

3. Coat thread with Super Glue or Zap-A-Gap.

4. For the overwing, tie in a sparse bunch of white bucktail in front of the eyes, extending over the top of the eyes and four times as long as the shank.

5. Add five strands of Krystal Flash, extending slightly beyond the bucktail.

6. Tie in a small bunch of olive bucktail under the hook and in front of the eyes. It should extend over the eyes the same length as the white bucktail.

7. Wrap thread in front of and behind the eyes. This constricts the bucktail and makes for a thin body profile.

8. Make a head.

9. Coat all thread wraps with epoxy.

**MATERIALS**
Hook: Gamakatsu Octopus hook, size 1/0
Thread: Clear monofilament
Tail: Silver Flashabou
Underwing: Chartreuse Ultrahair
Midwing: Peacock herl or peacock blue
   Flashabou
Overwing: Olive bucktail
Eyes: Orvis Cross-eyed Cone

**75**

GLASS MINNOW
*Tied by Gordon Churchill*

C apt. Gordon Churchill of North Carolina (www.flyfish-nc.com) developed this fly to mimic several species of baitfish called glass minnows. (These include spearing, sperling, and silversides.) He uses this imitation anytime he suspects game fish are feeding on glass minnows, and it has become his favorite fly for false albacore.

The finished fly should be sparse, suggesting a thin minnow you can nearly see through. His first versions were made with a head wrapped from Mylar, to which eyes were glued. He switched to Orvis Cross-eyed Cones because they're more durable and faster to work with.

Gordon arrived at the coloration for this fly by simple observation. When glass minnows get coughed up by fish being landed, they appear tan and drab—not at all like their live colors. But he once had a glass minnow jump out of the water and into the boat as it was being chased by something bigger with lots of teeth. He noticed the many colors of the live minnow, especially the chartreuse. That's when he decided to try the color combination shown here.

As an aside, Gordon notes that years ago, the winter after he first tied this pattern, he read about something similar to his pattern called the Ray's Fly. It was tied years before by Joe Brooks, proving that many "new" patterns have been around for many years in one form or another. However, it also proves that spending time observing natural baitfish or insects can lead to a pattern that's more effective than flies currently available—even if it resembles something that was created and then forgotten years earlier.

## TYING STEPS

1. Directly above the hook point, tie in 10 strands of silver Flashabou as a tail.

2. Just in front of the tail, tie in an underwing of 10 strands of chartreuse Ultrahair, the same length as the tail.

3. Just ahead of the underwing, add a midwing of 10 strands of peacock herl or peacock blue Flashabou, again as long as the tail.

4. Tie in an overwing of olive bucktail, not quite as long as the tail.

5. Tie in eyes and make a head.

**Materials**
Hooks: Gamakatsu Octopus circle hooks, 8/0
Thread: Monofilament
Wing: Green over yellow Super Hair
Throat: Yellow bucktail
Eyes: Silver 3-D molded
Head: 5-minute epoxy

## 76

### Billfish Baby
*Tied by Gary Graham*

For a trout fisherman like me, saltwater flies always hold a certain fascination. It's just hard to get your mind around the fact that these flies are often larger than the fish we catch in fresh water.

The Billfish Baby was developed by Gary Graham, who runs Baja On The Fly (www.bajafly.com) with his wife, Yvonne, in Mexico. Gary started working on this fly in 1999 while fishing for striped marlin at Magdalena Bay, where billfish numbering in the thousands gather to feed. The standard method is to tease them into fly-casting range with some kind of lure and then present a very large baitfish imitation on a fly rod. For many fishermen, casting these flies was like trying to throw a wet seagull.

Most of Gary's clients were showing up with traditional 12-inch, full-dress flies, which are often called "flop flies" because they can't be cast very far. Gary wanted a sparse fly, as light as possible, with hooks that are sharp right out of the box. He also wanted something that could be cast easily with a 14-weight rod.

Another change from the traditional flop flies was the use of circle hooks, which allow a hook-set in the corner of the fish's mouth most of the time. Also, many of the flop flies had two or three hook lengths between the two hooks. Gary shortened this distance so that the Billfish Baby's hooks were slightly more than one hook length apart (to satisfy IGFA record requirements).

The Billfish Baby is tied in several color combinations: green/yellow; blue/white; black/green; pink/white; red/orange; and purple/pink. The pattern worked so well on billfish that Gary began tying it on smaller hooks. It immediately proved successful on jacks, roosterfish, dorado, tuna, wahoo, and snook—quite a roster of saltwater heavyweights.

## TYING STEPS

1. Tie in green Super Hair to the stinger hook with the hook point up. The hair should be about 5 inches long.

2. On the bottom of the hook shank, tie in yellow Super Hair that is as long as the green.

3. Add a small bunch of yellow bucktail below the yellow Super Hair.

4. Attach the stinger hook to the front hook using 7-strand, 60-pound wire.

5. Move to the front hook and tie in a wing of green Super Hair. The length should extend as far back as the green tied on the stinger hook. The total length should be about 8 inches.

6. Tie in a throat of yellow bucktail just long enough to reach beyond the stinger hook.

7. Tie in some flash on each side.

8. Apply 3-D molded eyes.

9. Make a head of 5-minute epoxy. The epoxy should extend far enough back to prevent the hair from wrapping around the hooks.

## MATERIALS

Hook: Mustad 34007, sizes 1/0–2/0
Thread: Black monocord, 3/0
Tail: Black bunny strip and a few black
saddle hackles
Collar: Black Supreme Hair
Head: Black thread or Ultra Chenille
Eyes: Adhesive holographic
Epoxy: Devcon 5-minute epoxy

## 77

PUSHER Fly
*Tied by Jake Markezin*

This innovative pattern is the work of Jake Markezin from Fly Fish Pennsylvania (www.flyfishpa.net). Jake originally tied this fly for striped bass around the Jersey Shore.

The key to the Pusher is the ridged collar, which is created by flaring the Supreme Hair. The collar does two very important things. First, the cone-like shape permits movement of the bunny strip and saddle hackles while preventing them from wrapping around the hook. Second, the collar pushes water, which in turn creates noise that attracts striped bass.

Because Jake often uses this fly at night, he prefers an all-black version. The Pusher is especially effective when fished deep on a sinking line in the currents of an inlet or channel, where bass often hang low in the water column to pick off sand eels or other baitfish. In addition to stripers, he's also taken bluefish and weakfish on this fly during the nighttime bite.

## TYING STEPS

1. Lay down a thread base to the bend.

2. Tie in a 3- to 5-inch bunny strip.

3. Add a few saddle hackles.

4. Tie in a collar of Supreme Hair that encircles the bunny strip and extends well beyond the bend of the hook. When the collar hair is tied in small clumps on every side of the hook, it naturally flares out as you tighten the thread.

5. After the collar is secured, Zap-A-Gap it and then build a nice taper with thread or Ultra Chenille.

6. Add eyes.

7. Make a tapered head with epoxy.

# Steelhead and Salmon

**MATERIALS**
Hook: Alec Jackson Spey Fly, size 1½ (black)
Thread: Black, 6/0
Tail: Black bucktail and thin black saddle hackles
Head: Broad black Schlappen hackle tip
Eyes: Golden pheasant tippet, lacquered
Body: Black/purple Arizona Simi Seal
Rib: Langurtan tinsel, medium oval silver; long
    black saddle hackle
Back: Black golden pheasant wing or breast

**78**

FLATWING G. P.
*Tied by Dylan Rose*

"This fly should look like your hair after a long night with your buddies at a local pub," says Dylan Rose, who is a guide for Emerald Water Anglers (www.emeraldwateranglers.com) in Seattle, Washington. He reports that this fly is tied in the flat-wing style originated by East Coast striper guide Ken Abrames. It's now part of his standard steelhead arsenal.

This fly works well under all conditions on Northwest steelhead rivers. Due to its shagginess, it appears to come alive in the water. Dylan likes to fish the Flatwing G. P. on the swing through seams with moderate current. The dark saddles breathe and dance in the current, while the two eyes glow against the black body.

Sounds a little spooky to me, but you can't argue with success.

## Tying Steps

1. Tie in a sparse tail of long bucktail directly above the barb.

2. Tie in a dubbing pillow of soft downy feathers, the kind found at the base of a saddle hackle. This pillow will provide a base in which to lock the saddle hackles.

3. Tie in a tail of two skinny dry-fly hackles, tightening the stems into the dubbing pillow so they are flat against the shank. The concave side of the hackles should be facing down. These tails should be slightly longer than the length of the shank.

4. Tie in a broad, short saddle hackle tip on top of the long saddle hackles to form the "head." This short feather will hood the base of the saddles and lock them in place.

5. At this same point, tie in an orange golden pheasant tippet. Cut a "V" out of the tip to form two separate eyes.

6. Tie in the butt end of a long saddle hackle or Schlappen feather on the underside of the shank, just in front of the pillow.

7. At the same underside point, tie in a length of oval silver tinsel.

8. Dub a shaggy body halfway down the shank.

9. Wrap the tinsel forward of the body, but don't trim.

10. Wrap the saddle or Schlappen forward of the body, but don't trim.

11. Tie in a downward-curving golden pheasant feather to form the back.

12. Dub the body almost to the eye.

13. Advance the silver tinsel and then the remainder of the hackle. Clip the excess.

14. Tie in two more golden pheasant feathers for the back, layering one on top of the other.

15. Whip finish and cement the head.

## MATERIALS

Hook: Alec Jackson Spey, black, 3/0–7
Thread: Pearsall's Gossamer #35, salmonberry
Underlayment and Tag: Flat gold tinsel
Spey Hackle: Steelhead Anglers Spey Hackle,
  shrimp orange
Rib: Oval gold tinsel, 3/0–1.5 M, 3-5 S
Body: Alec Jackson Premium Silk Floss #29,
  peach
Collar: Gadwall, dyed shrimp orange
Wing: Bronze mallard

## 79

### SNOQUALMIE SPEY
*Tied by Jack Cook*

**S**pey flies are classics in the fly-fishing world, having been around since the 1850s. Their name is derived from the Scottish river where they were developed. This version of a spey fly was created by Jack Cook, who runs Steelhead Anglers (www.steelheadanglers.com) in Bellevue, Washington. He guides flyfishers on waters in Washington, Oregon, British Columbia, and even Russia. I wonder how he ever has time to tie flies...

The long soft fibers of the Snoqualmie Spey give the illusion of life, even in the slightest of currents. And clear water seems to be a requirement for this fly to work well. The first time Jack tried the Snoqualmie Spey, he was fishing down a run behind two other fly anglers. Those anglers had no hookups, but Jack's fly accounted for two fish in the same exact run. After talking Jack out of a couple of flies, they went back to the head of the run and were soon into fish of their own.

Most of the steelhead flies I've used here in the East have been bright, gaudy patterns, but Jack's experience in the Far West has been that the buggy flies have out-fished the gaudy patterns 10-to-1 over the years.

## TYING STEPS

1. Lay down a short thread base one-quarter the shank length behind the eye.

2. Tie in flat gold tinsel.

3. Wrap the tinsel back to a point above the barb and then up to where it started.

4. Trim the fibers from one side of the spey hackle. Strip a short section of the remaining butt-end fibers, leaving a bare stem to be wrapped over with thread.

5. Tie it in parallel to the shank with the fibers pointing back toward the bend.

6. Wrap the thread down to the bend where the first of the remaining spey hackles should be.

7. Tie in a length of oval tinsel for the rib.

8. Return the thread to the tie-in spot behind the eye.

9. Tie in silk and wrap it down to the bend and back.

10. Wrap the oval tinsel rib forward with no more than five turns and tie off.

11. Wrap the spey hackle up the shank and tie off near the eye.

12. Tie in the Gadwall by the tip and take two turns to make a collar. Tie off.

13. Tie in two wings of ¼-inch bronze mallard slips that reach to the hook point and sit on top of the body at a 45-degree angle.

**MATERIALS**
Hook: Mustad 79580, size 2
Thread: Black, 5/0
Body: Medium gold oval tinsel
Rib: Medium flat gold tinsel
Tail: Pheasant tail fibers
Wings: Gray squirrel, thin turkey
    strips, and deer body hair
Head: Brown deer hair

## 80

AUSTIN'S
BROWN MUddlER
*Tied by Austin Clark*

Work at something for 40 years and you'll probably get to be pretty good at it. So good, in fact, that people will hire you to do that thing. That's the way it is for Austin Clark, an Atlantic salmon guide with four decades of fishing behind him. He works with Lady Amherst, Inc. (www.ladyamherst.com), and was one of the first guides to recognize the importance of catch-and-release angling back in the days when it was virtually unheard of. In 2001, Austin was given the Atlantic Salmon Foundation's Honor Award, a very prestigious accolade.

Atlantic salmon are notoriously difficult to entice. Austin needed something to get his sports hooked up, and his solution was to adapt an existing pattern—the versatile Muddler Minnow—in an unusual way.

The flaring deer hair on the Austin's Brown Muddler is what makes this fly so effective. Austin reports that the hair opens up when the fly hits the water and when it's at rest between retrieves. He has his clients use it when they're sight fishing for Atlantics.

The Brown Muddler can be fished as a wet or as a dry. The fly really comes into its own when the water still isn't quite warm enough for dry flies. Stripping gives it the waking action that salmon seem to respond to so well.

## TYING STEPS

1. Tie in a tail of pheasant tail fibers at the bend.

2. Add a length of oval tinsel for ribbing.

3. Tie in flat gold tinsel and wind a body forward, leaving plenty of room to add the wings and head.

4. Make a wing of squirrel body hair that extends to the back of the tail.

5. Add thin strips of turkey tail segments on each side of the squirrel hair. These wings are much thinner and shorter than the wings on the standard Muddler.

6. Tie in a top wing of deer body hair. The hair must flare upward, away from the body. (This is opposite from the way the Muddler is usually tied.) The tips should reach beyond the bend.

7. Tie in an equally long bottom wing of deer body hair. The hair on the bottom of the body must flare downward, away from the body.

8. Begin spinning on deer body hair for the head.

9. Trim the head to a bullet shape, but make it thinner than you would on a traditional Muddler.

10. Whip finish and cement.

**81**

World's Simplest
Egg Fly
*Tied by Philip Krista*

Materials
  Hook: Mustad 9174, sizes 12–14
  Thread: Pink, 6/0
  Weight: Lead wire
  Yarn: Red Glo-Bug Yarn
  Yolk: Red permanent marker

Usually, I shy away from any fly with such a broad claim. In this case, however, I think it's worth taking a closer look. Philip Krista from Ellicott City, Maryland, guides around the globe and has probably seen most of what there is to see in the world of fly fishing.

The World's Simplest Egg Fly is his favorite egg pattern when nothing else is working. Fish it close to the bottom or below an indicator fly as part of a tandem rig.

I've met Philip at several fly-fishing shows and he's usually wearing a dress. Don't believe me? Check out his website at www.philipkrista.com. (It's actually a kilt, but he often refers to it as a dress.) He gives casting demonstrations with two-handed and spey rods.

At a recent show in Pennsylvania I had a chance to test one of his two-handed rods. It seemed like it was 18 feet long. Of course, he made the long casts look easy. I gave it a try, and I'm here to report that if you listen to his instructions you can get the fly out remarkable distances with only one false cast. How far? I'd say 100-foot casts are possible with just a little practice.

## Tying Steps

1. Make a few wraps of lead wire in the middle of the hook shank.

2. Bind the wire to the hook with several wraps of thread.

3. Attach a piece of Glo-Bug Yarn to the top and bottom of the hook.

4. Wrap tightly and make the yarn stand out from the hook.

5. Pick out the yarn to form a fuzzy ball.

6. Trim it into the shape of a small salmon egg.

7. Make a red dot on the top of the egg using a permanent marker.

**Materials**

Hook: Wilson 02 doubles, sizes 4–12
Thread: Black
Tag: Gold tinsel
Tail: Golden pheasant crest
Body: Back half of gold floss, front half of black floss
Rib: Gold tinsel
Throat: Hot orange calf tail
Wing: Black squirrel under green Krystal Hair
Head: Black thread

**82**

Kilbarry Stud
*Tied by Doug Lock*

Here's a pop quiz for you: What do The Moody Blues, Bad Company, Frank Zappa, Jimmy Page, and Motorhead have to do with fly fishing? The answer is Doug Lock. At one time or another, he was part of each of these rock bands. I guess all that jetting around and partying got old because he eventually found an extra kick from taking migratory fish on the fly. Now he runs a stud farm and instructs flyfishers in Ireland (www.speycast-ireland.com).

Doug needed a fly that worked on Atlantic salmon in peaty runoff conditions following storms on his home water, the Blackwater River. But what he developed works not only in off-color conditions, but also in clear water. The Kilbarry Stud takes its name from Doug's stud farm in Fermoy, County Cork.

He prefers to fish this pattern using a 9-foot leader and a 6-foot sink tip in front of a double-tapered floating line. How good is it? He reports that every spring salmon he's ever taken has fallen to the Kilbarry Stud. His pattern has accounted for salmon and seatrout in Ireland, Scotland, and Nova Scotia and dollaghan (a landlocked seatrout) in Northern Ireland.

Many of his spey-casting students have "broken their duck" on this pattern. I can only assume that this means the Kilbarry Stud brought them their first salmon.

## Tying Steps

1. Start with a double salmon hook, and tie in a tag of gold tinsel. Do not cut the tinsel off, as it will be used to rib the body.

2. Tie in a tail of golden pheasant crest extending three-quarters the length of the body. Set the crest so the natural curve of the feather points upward.

3. Tie on gold floss and wind a body half the length of the shank. Tie off and trim.

4. Tie in black floss and wind the front half of the body.

5. Wind the gold tinsel forward to make a rib for the body.

6. Make a throat of hot orange calf tail. It should extend to the point of the hook.

7. Make a wing of black squirrel, and then add a sparse bunch of green Krystal Hair over the squirrel. On sizes 4 and 6, top this with a long golden pheasant crest curving downward over the body.

8. Make a head, whip finish, and cement.

**83**

*Tied by Loren Williams*

Materials
Hook: Mustad 80250, sizes 8–16
Thread: Pink, 6/0
Tail (optional): Three to five short
strands of cerise Krystal Flash
Body: One ply of pink Sparkle Yarn

In the springtime, a young man's fancy turns to thoughts of...spawning suckers. At least according to Loren Williams, who runs the Fly Guy's Flies and Guide Service (www.flyguysoutfitting.com) in Port Byron, New York. Apparently the fancy of trout, steelhead, chinook, and coho also turn toward spawning suckers, but for a different reason. With all those game fish following suckers around for their roe, it's a miracle that any hatch out at all.

Loren notes that there are many variations for this pattern. He settled on Sparkle Yarn because of its multi-ply construction and intrinsically subtle flash. Most of his salmon and steelhead flies look like eggs, so this simple pattern fits the bill nicely. Loren likes his clients to get their flies down on the bottom with a dead drift, but many flies are lost with this method. Because this fly takes less than a minute to tie, he has no second thoughts about fishing deep.

In addition to the color shown here, other good options include white, cream, gold, and orange. Tie a few of each with and without tails. On bright days when fish are spawning, a fly with a Krystal Flash tail usually out-produces one tied without a tail. However, when Loren is fishing for holdover steelhead after the spawning season is over he gets more action using a tailless fly in a more subdued color. He thinks this is because the muted colors better imitate the water-hardened eggs the fish are still eating.

## Tying Steps

1. Lay down a thread base from behind the eye to a spot just above the hook point.

2. Cut a length of Sparkle Yarn and separate the yarn into single-ply strands.

3. Tie in a tail of Krystal Flash that's equal in length to the hook shank.

4. Tie in the Sparkle Yarn where the Krystal Flash was tied in.

5. Make a smallish loop with the yarn and secure it with two or three turns of thread.

6. Continue making loops as you move toward the eye. Each loop should be offset from the last, and slightly larger. This technique makes a tapered body that covers the shank from side to side. The number and size of the loops are up to you. More loops on a larger hook can look like a hunk of fresh skein while fewer loops on a smaller hook can look like a single egg.

7. Secure the yarn behind the eye.

8. Make a head and whip finish.

**MATERIALS**
Hook: Mustad 9672, sizes 6–8
Thread: Black, 6/0
Body: Green tinsel
Wing: White calf tail

**84**

MIKE'S LITTLE
GREEN THING
*Tied by Mike Gallion*

Little green things aren't typically good items to have around, but you'll probably want to make an exception for Mike Gallion's Little Green Thing. Mike runs Fish Creek Flyer Guide Service (www.magnumss.com) in and around the Juneau area of southeast Alaska. He had been searching for a fly that would be effective on several different species, easy to fish, and fast enough to tie that he wouldn't blow a whole night whipping up a couple dozen. This fly is what he came up with.

So just how did this fly get its name? Actually, it was never really given a name. It sort of acquired one in the field; as in, "Whatcha usin'? One of Mike's little green things?" The fly's loyal followers have shortened it to LGT.

The fly has been used successfully on most Pacific salmon, including pinks, chum, cohos, and chinooks. He's also caught flounder, baby halibut, sculpin, Dolly Varden, cutthroat trout, eels, and yellow perch with it.

As if that's not enough, this fly was, at one time or another, responsible for seven IGFA tippet-class records and one IGFA all-tackle record. The records were on pink and chum salmon and starry flounder. The big flounder came up off the bottom while Mike was fishing for chums. He's not sure who was more surprised, the flounder or him. The most recent record, taken near Juneau, was a 17-pound chum on 6-pound tippet.

Mike reports one interesting aspect of this fly's performance: When it doesn't work, it *really* doesn't work. I've had lots of days like that myself, so I know what he means. He says he's practically beaten Lahontan cutthroats over the head with it, but they completely ignore it. Thankfully, there are plenty of other species out there that eat it like candy.

## Tying Steps

1. Tie in some green tinsel behind the eye. Wrap a body back beyond the bend of the hook and up to the starting point again. Be sure the body extends far down the bend of the hook. (Does it make a difference if the body doesn't extend down the bend? Yes. Mike has done a lot of experimenting and insists this step makes for a more effective fly.)

2. Tie in a sparse wing of white calf tail, not too long. It should be symmetrical, with the longest fibers in the center of the wing and the shorter ones above and below.

3. Make a head, whip finish, and cement.

**MATERIALS**
Hook: Mustad 800700 BR, size 10
Thread: Chartreuse, 6/0
Bead: Rainbow, 3mm
Tail: Alaskan roe orange Glo-Bug Yarn
Body: Chartreuse Estaz

**85**

CANDY CORN
*Tied by Morris Kashuba*

Morris Kashuba (570-489-9525) from Peckville, Pennsylvania, has been a fly tier for the better part of 30 years. One of his most famous patterns is the Rainbow Bead Fly. Morris's flies are used on many Lake Ontario tributaries for rainbows, lakers, steelhead, browns, and salmon. Poke around in an upstate New York fly shop and you'll likely come across his creations.

The key to the Candy Corn is the plastic rainbow bead, which has a multi-colored finish. As is often the case, the novelty of this color may account for its success. Sometimes showing fish something different can put you over the top when it comes to taking heavily pressured species. The fish see all kinds of patterns and wise up fairly quickly. Drift something new over them and curiosity often puts them on the hook.

Another important aspect of the plastic bead is that it floats. This keeps the fly just off the bottom and in the fish's strike zone. Remember, migrating fish will seldom chase a fly, so getting it down in their faces is necessary to trigger a strike. This pattern can be fished either with a small split shot or on a sinking line. The favored technique is a swinging down-and-across presentation.

Candy Corn is not the only color variation of this fly. Morris has several body/collar combinations: the Pink Lady, with chartreuse/opal hot pink; Blue Wing, with purple/opal dark blue; Black Bird, with black and chartreuse twist/black; the Oyster Shell, with hot pink/pearl; Lady Pearl, with chartreuse/opal pearl; Shrimp, with Uni-Glow #12/light pink; and the Egg Drift, with orange/opal salmon. Some days, one will work when others won't. As the fish aren't talking, we'll probably never know why. Just keep testing the various color combinations until you find one the fish want.

If you're fishing for migratory species in the Great Lakes tributaries, you'll be happy you have this fly along in a variety of colors. I suspect it'll work very well during the West Coast anadromous runs, too.

## TYING STEPS

1. Slide a rainbow bead up to the eye.

2. Tie in Glo-Bug Yarn at the bend of the hook for a tail and body.

3. Trim the tail short.

4. Tie in a length of Estaz.

5. Wrap the yarn forward to the bead and tie off.

6. Wrap the Estaz over the yarn body to the bead and tie off.

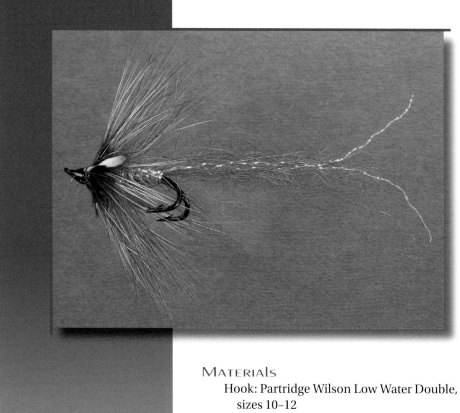

**MATERIALS**

Hook: Partridge Wilson Low Water Double,
sizes 10–12
Thread: Black silk
Tail: Orange calf tail and green Krystal Flash
Rib: Silver tinsel
Body: Black silk thread, read one-third; gold
silk floss, front two-thirds
Hackle: Orange cock, badger cock
Cheeks: Jungle cock

**86**

**KilbARRY ShRimp**
*Tied by Doug Lock*

A tlantic salmon have a well-earned reputation for being particular about what they'll eat. So when Doug Lock (www.speycast-ireland.com) wanted a red "autumn" pattern to fish in the "streamy" water at the heads and tails of salmon pools, he knew it had to be a special fly. The Kilbarry Shrimp is what he created.

The double cock hackles of this fly give it the appearance of mobility. The fly looks totally different once it's in the water. Although Doug named it as a shrimp, he's sure it resembles a small squid, with the large jungle cock eyes similar to the prominent eyes of a squid. Doug believes this likeness sparks an instinctive strike that harks back to the salmon's time feeding at sea.

One particular day early in the history of this fly stands out in Doug's memory. He was instructing a party from France when they asked him for a demonstration of spey casting as they enjoyed their lunch on the riverbank. He tied on the Kilbarry Shrimp, and within seconds of the fly hitting the water on the first cast, he felt a very gentle take. He let the fish run with the fly and the current set the hook. He soon landed an 11-pound salmon. Not a bad way to start. Needless to say, his clients were impressed and went on to have great success with this fly.

The Kilbarry Shrimp has produced double-digit fish for Doug in Ireland, and others have done well with it on the Miramichi and on salmon rivers in Norway and Scotland. Doug usually fishes this fly on a floating line with a section of sink tip added. But another angler fished it on the river Spey in Scotland on a full floating line and, because of the cock hackles, the fly didn't sink. A grilse took it right on the surface.

## TYING STEPS

1. Start with a double salmon hook and tie in a length of silver tinsel for ribbing.

2. Tie in a tail of orange calf tail and green Krystal Flash that extends twice the length of the body.

3. Wrap a thread body extending one-third of the way to the eye.

4. Tie on gold silk floss and wind the forward two-thirds of the body. Tie off and trim.

5. Wind the silver tinsel forward to make a rib for the body.

6. Tie in a hackle collar of orange cock.

7. Tie in a second hackle collar of badger cock.

8. Tie on jungle cock eyes.

9. Make a head, whip finish, and cement.

**87**

Guides'
Steelhead Fly
*Tied by Bob Rock*

Materials
Hook: Mustad R72 Long Nymph,
2X heavy and long, sizes 6–12
Thread: Black, 6/0
Body: Black chenille
Tail: Goose biots
Wing Case: Black Swiss Straw
Thorax: Root beer Estaz

Now, if you're an English teacher as well as a flyfisher, don't get all bent out of shape because you think I misused the plural possessive. The reason for this questionable usage comes from Bob Rock (rwrock@dreamscape.com) in Oswego, New York. It seems that at least four Salmon River guides claim to have invented or named this fly. Ergo, Bob calls it the Guides' Fly. If so many pros want to claim it, it must be worth considering.

Bob says steelhead world-record holder and Salmon River fly-fishing pioneer Fran Verdoliva showed this fly to him several years ago. (Fran is now the Salmon River Corridor Coordinator for New York State, and many anglers insist that no one knows the Salmon better than he does.) Fran's clients had numerous hookups and had landed several fish on a day where Bob had gone fishless—until Fran was kind enough to give him a few of these flies. After that, Bob's success rate improved dramatically.

Sight fishing is a favorite technique with this fly. Once he spots a fish, Bob likes to set up directly opposite, about 15 to 20 feet away. He flips the fly upstream just far enough so that it has time to get down to the same depth as the fish. When the fly stops, it's time to tighten up quickly but gently. If Bob can feel the fish's head shaking, he'll sweep the rod directly downstream and set the hook. If the line stops but there is no head shaking, the fish may be foul-hooked. Throwing a little slack line will usually cause the hook to fall off.

These days, the thorax is tied with red, black, orange, or chartreuse Estaz. But Bob's favorite is root beer.

The Guides' Fly is very effective on Pacific salmon that spawn in Lake Ontario tributaries. Bob thinks the fly resembles the abundant stoneflies in the Salmon River. In his experience, smaller flies seem to work better closer to the estuary, while larger patterns are preferred near the headwaters.

## Tying Steps

1. Tie in a thread base starting at the eye and ending over the point of the hook.

2. Build up a small bump at the end of the thread base to splay the tails.

3. Tie in a goose biot on either side of the bump to make the tail. The biots should be about as long as the hook shank.

4. Tie in the chenille for the body by wrapping to the eye and back down half the length of the body. Tie off.

5. Tie in 1 inch of Swiss Straw, with the butt pointing toward the hook eye.

6. Tie in a length of Estaz and wrap it forward three or four turns to create a thorax. Tie off.

7. Tightly pull the standing Swiss Straw over the thorax and tie it off. Trim the excess.

8. Make a small thread head, whip finish, and cement.

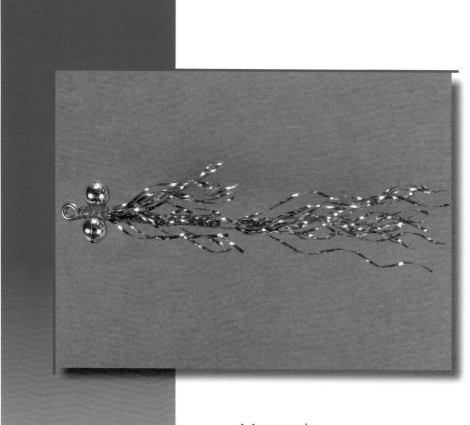

## MATERIALS

Hook: Eagle Claw D1197 DF, gold
   finish, sizes 2–4
Thread: Red, 2/0
Tail, Body, and Collar: Braided Mylar
   tinsel, silver, gold, red, or green
Eyes: Bead chain

## 88

### CAPTAIN COMET
*Tied by Tony Lolli*

The rocks have teeth on the Salmon River in New York. My clients are pretty good at feeding those rocks when they aren't fast to fish, so I like flies that are effective but simple. The Comet, originally designed for steelhead and Pacific salmon, has evolved into a great general pattern. Most variations are easy to tie, and this one is no exception.

Salmon are aggressive when just starting their run and don't much seem to care what you put in front of them, so it makes sense to use something quick, easy, and cheap to tie. The Captain Comet has worked so well for me that it's the only fly I use for Pacific salmon on the Salmon River. I've also used it with great success in British Columbia.

Sight fishing is my favorite style in New York. It's exciting and has put my clients fast to some nice fish. Stand opposite the fish and drift the fly through the lie at the fish's depth. When the line stops, gently tighten up.

## Tying Steps

1. Start with a stout, long-shanked hook.

2. The tail, body, and collar are formed from a single piece of braided Mylar tinsel that measures three times the length of the hook shank. Pull out and discard the core. I put my closed scissors into the braiding and gently open them to separate the Mylar strands.

3. Unbraid the tail section to one and a half times the shank length. At the other end, unbraid half the shank length for the collar.

4. Next, thread the Mylar over the eye and onto the shank. Tie the body onto the shank at the start of the bend with some 2/0 thread; tie off and cut the thread.

5. Gently tighten the braid by pulling it forward and tie the body in at the eye.

6. Fold the collar fibers back over the hook and tie down.

7. Tie in two bead-chain eyes on top of the hook. The bead eyes make the fly ride with the point up and discourage all but the hungriest rocks.

8. Cement all wrappings.

## Materials

Hook: Tiemco 5263, 3XL and 2X heavy, size 4
Thread: Black monocord, 3/0
Beads: Red plastic, ⅜ inch
Cement: Softex epoxy
Tail: Black marabou
Body: Black crosscut Zonker strips
Head Cement: Zap-A-Gap

**89**

Double Beadhead
Black Egg-Sucking
Epoxy Leech
*Tied by Rick Hedding*

Yikes! It takes more time to pronounce this fly's name than it does to tie it. The pattern comes courtesy of Rick Hedding of Family Christian Anglers (509-869-1444 or www.familychristiananglers.com) in Spokane, Washington. It's his go-to fly for steelhead when the water is above 45 degrees.

Rick originated this design many years ago while fishing in Alaska's famous Iliamna drainage. He's also used it for trout in many Montana rivers, and he now uses it while guiding in Washington State. The most unusual thing about this fly is the method for mounting the beads.

He generally fishes the fly on a traditional wet-fly swing, quartering his casts across and fishing down on a sink-tip line. Another method is to use a floating line with a split shot and strike indicator for dead-drift fishing. Cast straight upstream and allow the rig to drift without any drag. Rick's only warning is to use a 2X or 3X tippet because big fish strike this fly savagely.

## Tying Steps

1. With the hook in the vise, heat the eye area with a flame until it's red hot. Quickly force the first bead over the eye and down the shank until you have enough room for the second bead.

2. Reheat, if necessary, and force the second bead over the eye.

3. Quickly push both beads up against the eye before the hook cools off.

4. After it cools, remove the hook and dip the front end into Softex epoxy until both beads are covered. Be sure to clean out the hook eye with a bodkin.

5. Let the epoxy dry for 20 minutes and repeat the dipping process. Two coats are perfect.

6. Hang the fly to dry and prepare more hooks and beads in the same way, as it's much easier to tie this fly in bunches. Come back to them when you're ready to dress the rest of the fly.

7. When the epoxy is dry, place the hook back in the vise and lay down a thread base to the bend of the hook.

8. Tie in a full tail of marabou as long as the body.

9. Tie in a Zonker strip with the material facing backwards. Palmer the strip forward until it crowds the beads.

10. Whip finish and use Zap-A-Gap on the threads.

**MATERIALS**
Hook: Mustad 3906, size 4
Thread: Red, 4/0
Body: White marabou
Shoulder: Wood duck flank feather fibers

## 90

### SUPER SECRET
### SALMON SLAYER
*Tied by Brett Damm*

Super secret? Well, not anymore. What was Brett Damm thinking when he let this cat out of the bag? Brett runs the River to Ridge Guide Service (207-966-2885 or www.maineguides.com/members/rivertoridge) in Hebron, Maine. Like most guides, he has a favorite searching pattern for times when the fishing gets tough, and this is it. You'll need to pay close attention to the tying instructions for this pattern because the methods are a little different than what most tiers are accustomed to.

Brett modified a traditional marabou streamer to create the Salmon Slayer. The problem with the original fly was that salmon tended to strike short at the flowing marabou tail. He decided to balloon the body to give the fly more bulk, causing the fish to strike farther up and increasing hookups.

He uses this pattern in the fast water at the heads of pools and in pocket water. It can be fished by retrieving straight up against the current or by casting down and across. When fishing with the latter method you should strip the fly fast near the end of the swing so it ferries quickly across the top of the water.

This fly also comes into its own below dams. Here, the fly is fished on a dead drift to salmon that are used to feeding on injured baitfish. A split shot can be added to get the fly down when necessary.

## Tying Steps

1. Wrap a short thread base at the bend of the hook. Tie off and cut, leaving a 6-inch tag end hanging from the bend for use later.

2. Tie in next to this short thread base and wrap a new thread base two-thirds of the way to the hook eye.

3. Prepare a marabou feather by finding the point where the longest fibers start growing from the stem.

4. Strip off all the shorter fibers and discard. Only the longest fibers remain, and they reach all the way to the tip of the feather.

5. Trim the bare stem to the point where the long fibers start growing.

6. Tie in the marabou one-third the shank length back from the eye. The feather should be tied in with the concave side facing up.

7. Palmer the marabou forward toward the eye. Be sure to tease the fibers back toward the bend after every wrap. You should have a fuzzy-looking bush with the fibers standing away from the hook.

8. Tie off the marabou stem and cut the excess.

9. Make shoulders from wood duck fibers on each side of the fly. These should be no longer than the length of the shank.

10. Make a head and finish it off.

11. Stroke the marabou fibers back until all the fibers are smoothed out toward the back, and then hold them in place. At this point, the fly should look like a traditional marabou streamer.

12. With your left hand, grasp the fibers at the bend and push them toward the eye so they balloon up over the hook shank. Now the body is shaped something like a Sparkle Pupa emerger.

13. Use the hanging tag end of the thread left in step 1 to tie the marabou fibers down to the shank at the bend. This leaves the body ballooned up and the tail sticking out about two shank lengths beyond the bend.

14. Cement all the wraps.

**MATERIALS**
Hook: Mustad 80400, sizes 4–10
Thread: White, 6/0
Weight: Lead wire, .30
Body: Pearl Diamondbraid
Upper and Lower Wings: White Zonker strips
Accent Flash: Pearl Flashabou
Eyes: Prismatic stick-on eyes
Head: Two coats of 5-minute epoxy

## 91

WHITE
DOUBLEBUNNY
*Tied by Loren Williams*

If one is good, then two must be better. At least that's what I assume Loren Williams was thinking when he created this pattern. Loren runs Fly Guy's Flies and Guide Service (www.flyguysoutfitting.com) in Port Byron, New York.

The interesting thing about this pattern is the way he added a flashy body to the original pattern to make it more effective. The Diamondbraid creates a more realistic appearance than the original hide-to-hide pattern, and it also allows weight to be incorporated.

Loren reports that this is a very versatile pattern that can be fished by anglers of any experience level. He fishes it in traditional streamer style upstream, across, and downstream. He also fishes it dead drift below a strike indicator. Browns, steelhead, and salmon suck the fly in as it passes by or chase it crosscurrent—it doesn't seem to matter.

If two are better than one, I wonder how a Quadruplebunny would work.

## TYING STEPS

1. Weight the middle two-thirds of the hook with turns of lead wire.

2. Cover the wire with thread, being sure to taper both ends.

3. Tie in a strip of Diamondbraid behind the eye and bind it down along the entire length of the shank to a spot just above the hook's point. Move the thread behind where the Diamondbraid is tied in.

4. Cut a length of Zonker strip equal to the length of the shank plus the hook gape. This makes for a short tail that will not foul around the hook.

5. Separate the hair at the point where the tail will begin and tie the Zonker strip in securely where the Diamondbraid ends.

6. Advance the thread to the eye.

7. Wrap the Diamondbraid in close wraps toward the eye to form a body over the lead wire.

8. Pull the Zonker strip tightly over the top of the body and secure with thread. Trim excess.

9. Turn the hook over.

10. Cut a second length of Zonker strip the same size as the first.

11. Poke the hook point through the hide side of the strip, leaving enough to match the upper tail. Slide the strip along the bend until it meets the upper Zonker strip. Do not tie it down. It will be held in place by the pressure created when it's pulled toward the eye.

12. Pull the strip forward and tie off behind the eye at the same location as the first strip.

13. Tie in four or five strands of Flashabou on each side of the fly. Clip the strips to different lengths.

14. Build a broad tapered head and attach stick-on eyes where the fur, thread, and Flashabou meet.

15. Give the head and eyes two coats of 5-minute epoxy or waterproof cement.

## Materials
Hook: Mustad 80200BR shrimp/caddis,
sizes 6–10 (salmon) and 10–12
(steelhead and trout)
Thread: Copper wire
Red Dubbing Mix: Red beaver, red angora,
and red flash
Black Dubbing Mix: Black beaver, black
angora, and black flash

## 92

Tom's 60-Second
Red Head
*Tied by Randy Jones*

One fly for all seasons and all species? Well, maybe not every species, but for Pacific salmon, steelhead, and brown trout in New York's Salmon River, this is the go-to fly of Randy Jones of The Yankee Angler (www.yankeeangler.com). It all depends on which species is running at the time. As an added bonus, this fly takes only 60 seconds to tie; hence, the name. That's an important feature when you're a guide with clients who are hooking up many times each day and losing lots of flies as a result.

Randy has some thoughts on why this egg-sucking nymph pattern out-fishes all others on a consistent basis: (1) the angora dubbing gets caught in the fish's teeth during the take, giving the angler more time to detect the strike; (2) the spiky angora fibers move in the water, giving the appearance of live action; and (3) the flash gives off a subtle reflection unlike the gaudier materials often used for these species. This last point can be especially important on bright days, when fish often become fly-shy after many days of heavy angling pressure. In low, clear water, when other flashy flies send the fish racing upstream, this pattern won't frighten them. Also, the wire adds enough weight to get the fly to the bottom quickly, which is where these species strike.

Randy likes using wire and notes that other colors can be used to imitate other insects. Green wire, along with a small black head, works as a caddis larva pattern. Natural copper wire with brown dubbing and a small black head looks like a cased caddis. Natural copper and a peacock herl head imitates a midge pupa (e.g., Brassie). Or try all black for a stonefly nymph. All brown works for a mayfly nymph. An all-orange pattern is called an O. J., and Randy says it's a killer.

## Tying Steps

1. In place of thread, wrap the shank with copper wire, ending just past the bend of the hook.

2. Apply black dubbing to the wire and wrap a tapered body, stopping three-quarters of the way to the eye. Keep a slender profile and don't over-dub the body.

3. Apply red dubbing and wrap an "egg" ahead of the body. The egg should be thick and one-quarter the length of the black body. The red head's size should vary according to the size of the natural eggs in the river you're planning to fish.

4. Half-hitch the wire, pull tight, and snap it off. Don't worry about the fly coming apart. It won't.

**MATERIALS**
Hook: Mustad 9672, sizes 2–8
Thread: Black, 6/0
Weight (optional): Lead wire
Rib: Flat gold tinsel, size 14
Body: Olive dun Antron yarn, Umpqua AY162
Throat: White calf tail, under golden pheasant crest
Wing: Gray calf tail, peacock herl, and gray
    marabou
Cheek: Silver pheasant
Eyes (optional): Jungle cock

**93**

**SILVER GHOST**
*Tied by Joe Catalano*

Sometimes "oldies but goodies" live on forever, although in this particular case, the oldie needed a little help to become even more effective.

Joe Catalano (978-686-0487) guides in New Hampshire, not far from Maine's Richardson Lake. It was here that Ms. Carrie Stevens invented the Gray

Ghost many years ago. It's a fly that remains in use today in northern New England and other areas around the country.

Just a little farther west are the headwaters of the Connecticut River, where Joe guides regularly. He made some changes to Stevens's pattern to better match the local baitfish there. The first change was the use of green Antron for the lateral line. Next, he replaced the wing of saddle hackle with marabou to improve the action.

Joe reports that the fly should be fished using different methods to match the season. In the spring, he fishes it in the traditional way, down and across the current. However, in the fall he dead-drifts it until it starts to swing, then strips it back upstream. This area of the Connecticut River has several bottom-release dams, and when the lakes turn over in the fall, baitfish living there are dragged through the outflow of the dams. They enter the river dead or dazed, which is what makes dead-drifting so effective in the fall.

Legendary flies achieve their status for good reasons, but sometimes a few minor adjustments are all it takes to make them even more productive.

## Tying Steps

1. Tie in just in front of the bend.

2. Tie in gold tinsel at the bend, with the tag pointing toward the back.

3. Advance the thread almost to the eye.

4. Tie in olive dun Antron yarn and wrap it to the bend and back over itself to the starting point.

5. Wrap the tinsel halfway down the bend and back over itself to where the back of the Antron body ends.

6. Make evenly spaced wraps of tinsel over the Antron and tie off behind the eye.

7. Tie in a sparse amount of white calf tail as a throat, extending to the hook point.

8. Tie in a golden pheasant crest under the calf tail, also extending to the hook point.

9. Add an underwing of white calf tail on top of the hook.

10. Tie in four strands of peacock herl over the underwing and extending past the bend.

11. Tie in gray marabou as an overwing. The length should be one to two hook gapes beyond the bend.

12. Add silver pheasant cheeks one-third the length of the body.

13. Add jungle cock eyes.

14. Make a head, whip finish, and coat with black lacquer.

## MATERIALS

Hook: Gamakatsu steelhead streamer, sizes
4–1/0
Weight (optional): Lead wire
Thread: Chartreuse Uni-Thread or chartreuse
Kevlar, 3/0
Tail and Rear Body: Cerise fuchsia, cerise, or hot
pink straight-cut bunny strip
Mid-Body: Crosscut hot orange bunny strip
Forward Body: Crosscut chartreuse bunny strip
Head: Chartreuse marabou blood quill
Mid-Flash: Fuchsia Flashabou strands
Forward-Flash: Prismatic holographic Krystal
Flash

## 94

GERRY GARCIA
*Tied by Gordy Gracey*

G erry Garcia lives! The very first time Gordy Gracey of Fishing Northwest (www.fishingnorthwest.com) in Forks, Washington, suggested his client try this new fly, the client raised an eyebrow and asked what hallucinogenic Gordy was smoking when he invented it. But soon the fellow was into his very first steelhead, and he gave the psychedelic fly its name.

Gordy had seen many steelies caught on bright red, green, and pink hard baits. He designed this fly to incorporate these colors, yet have the form of natural forage.

The fly works best on fresh incoming steelhead, usually those in the lower sections of a river. Gordy likes to fish it in 2 to 5 feet of water in tailouts and riffles. He fishes it with a traditional swing: tight line and static profile presentation, with a hang-down at the end of the drift.

## Tying Steps

1. Lay down a thread base that starts ¼ inch behind the hook eye and ends ⅛ inch before the bend.

2. Apply a coat of head cement to create a solid base.

3. Tie in a fuchsia, cerise, or hot pink bunny fur strip parallel to the hook shank with three or four tight wraps, leaving 1 inch hanging out as a tail. Advance the thread one-third of the way up the hook shank.

4. Wrap the fur strip in close, non-overlapping wraps to the thread. Tie off and cut the fur strip.

5. Tie in the tag end of a hot orange bunny strip where the first bunny strip ended.

6. Wrap forward over another one-third of the shank. Tie off and trim.

7. Tie in 10 pieces of Flashabou on each side of the hook. The pieces should be ½ inch shorter than the tail.

8. Tie in the tag end of a chartreuse bunny strip and wrap forward to within ¼ inch of the eye. Tie off and trim.

9. Spin on a generous amount of holographic (clear) Krystal Flash evenly around the shank. It should be the length of the shank and should lay back against the hook. Trim the excess away from the eye.

10. Take two wraps of chartreuse marabou.

11. Make a head, whip finish, and cement.

## MATERIALS

Hook: Tiemco 7999 streamer, size 4
Thread: Black Kevlar
Tail: Black marabou, Krystal Flash, and
    pink marabou
Body: Red and black Krystal Flash
    chenille, palmered with black hackle
Head: Orange yarn

## 95

### BUFFET TABLE EGGS
### (SUCKING LEECH)
*Tied by Bob Nall*

Bob Nall (208-756-2264) guides steelhead anglers for several outfitters on four hundred miles of the Salmon River from the headwaters near Stanley, Idaho, to the Snake River confluence near Lewiston. The steelhead season runs from September through April, and this is his go-to fly for most conditions.

He had been looking for something that would tempt the fish the way a buffet line tempts you and me. His pattern has a little bit of everything, and based on its track record the steelies really seem to like it. We know that steelhead don't really eat much during the run, and the ones that reach central Idaho have been on the road for a long time. But this fly apparently sparks some instinct the fish can't control. In fact, during one day of the testing phase, the Fish & Game agent at the check station told Bob he caught the only fish that day.

Bob uses spey rods and sink-tip lines to cast to mid-current, with a good upstream mend to allow the fly to get down quickly. After the fly swings toward shore, he works it back up with strips. When landing fish, he's noticed that the yarn often hangs up in their teeth, which probably gives him a fraction of a second longer to set the hook on the take.

Every guide has to think of a gracious way to convince his clients that they need to use the pro's recommended techniques if they want to hook up. When his clients ignore his advice and just fish the way they usually do, Bob has a solution. He fishes along behind them, hooking fish the client has missed. That's usually enough to convince them to try the recommended tactics and Buffet Table Eggs.

## Tying Steps

1. Tie in a thread base to the hook bend.

2. Tie in a tail of black marabou, and add a few strands of Krystal Flash and pink marabou.

3. Tie in a hackle to be palmered later.

4. Tie in one strand of red Krystal Flash chenille and one strand of black. Twist the two and wrap forward three-quarters of the way to the eye. This creates a body with alternating red and black segmentation.

5. Wind the hackle forward and tie off.

6. Make a large head of orange yarn.

7. Whip finish and cement.

# WARM WATER

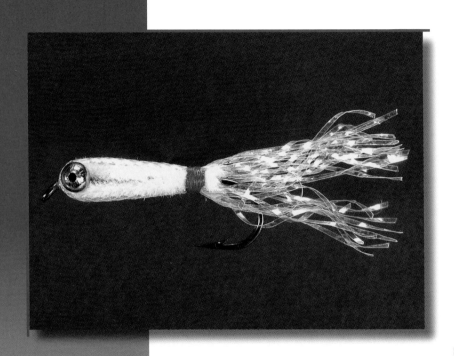

## Materials

Hook: Mustad 9672, sizes 2–8
Thread: Red, 6/0
Tail: Teased out Mylar tube, size small,
   as long as the hook shank
Body: Looped medium Ultra Chenille
Eyes: Small silver bead chain
Overbody: Small Mylar tube pulled
   over the eyes and tied in back

## 96

### Cypert's
### Mylar Minnow
*Tied by Mike Hogue*

This Mylar Minnow is the creation of Mike Hogue of Badger Creek Fly Tying (www.eflytier.com) in Freeville, New York. Mike has given demonstrations and lectures at many regional and national fly-fishing shows, and his articles have appeared in a variety of publications.

Mike was visiting with Texas guide Charlie Cypert some time back and became interested in Charlie's pencil poppers. The Mylar Minnow emerged from that study. Mike uses this fly primarily for crappie and smallmouth and largemouth bass, but it has also taken trout, stripers, redfish, weakfish, and even carp. Now that carp are getting such increased attention from flyfishers these days, you might want to arm yourself with a few Mylar Minnows and give them a try.

Mike explains that since this is a baitfish pattern, swimming the fly is important. He fishes down and across the current, allowing the fly to sink slowly, and he retrieves it will small, deliberate strips. Adding to the attractiveness of this fly is the fact that it sinks slowly and has a good action on the retrieve. And its color makes it easy to see in murky water.

The method used to attach the materials for this fly is different than what you may have seen before, so follow the instructions carefully. There is also a variation of this fly designed for steelhead and salmon that incorporates Estaz. Instead of looping the Estaz, wrap it around the shank before adding the Mylar tubing.

## Tying Steps

1. Make figure-eight wraps to position the bead-chain eyes on top of the hook and Super Glue the eyes in position. Cut the thread off.

2. Retie the thread above the bend.

3. Loop a length of Vernille (Ultra Chenille) over one of the chain eyes so the ends of the loop are at the rear of the hook shank, and tie down at the bend. Repeat for the other eye. This gives you four strands of Vernille running along the sides of the shank, two strands on each side. Trim the ends.

4. Lay a strip of Mylar tubing over the hook eye. Pull the Mylar over the chain eyes by forcing the braid over the hook eye and tie at back. In other words, the braid is pulled onto the hook doubled over, with half on top and half on the bottom. The braid runs through the eye and is only tied in at the bend of the hook. The braid should extend beyond the bend a distance equal to the length of the hook shank.

5. Tease out the braided ends for a tail. The tail and top and bottom of the fly are all created from one piece of Mylar tube.

**MATERIALS**
Hook: Eagle Claw 254SS or
    Mustad 3407, sizes 2/0–3/0
Thread: Size A for bulk
Tail: White Zonker strip
Body: Tinsel stem
Wing: White bucktail
Topping: Silver tinsel
Eye: Prism eyes

**97**

PIKER BUNNY
*Tied by Ed Marsh*

Tell the truth. If you saw this fly hanging from a waterside tree branch, would you bother to stop and pick it up? Doubtful. That's what I love about guide flies: they're designed to catch fish, not fishermen. Now, suppose there was a sign next to the fly explaining that this pattern has accounted for more than 2,500 pike since 1960. Would that change your mind?

The Piker Bunny comes from Ed Marsh of Colorado Springs, Colorado. This is not his first fly creation, either. He's responsible for a couple of other patterns you probably remember reading about in *Field & Stream* magazine: the Miracle Nymph and the Buckskin Nymph.

According to Ed, pike are not the dummies anglers often assume them to be. He's found that they will ignore patterns they've seen before but jump on something new or different. That's why Ed keeps experimenting with different color combinations for this pattern. His favorite tail/wing colorations include all white, white and red, black and yellow, and black and red. The body colors he uses include gold, silver, red, green, blue, and purple.

Fishing this pattern effectively requires a little bit of on-the-water experimentation. You can't tell in advance which type of retrieve will trip the pike's trigger on any given day. Ed suggests varying the retrieve from fast to slow to full stop. Sometimes the fish even hit the fly as it sinks or when the retrieve is stopped.

This is a seasonal fly; it's at its best when pike are working the shallows. In Colorado, the best months are May through July. Ed also notes that the best time of day for pike fishing is usually from noon until 5 or 6 PM. By then, the shallows have warmed into the 60-degree range.

Most of the materials are available through traditional fly-tying supply outlets, but Ed picks up the tinsel stems for the body at craft stores.

## TYING STEPS

1. Lay down a thread base and tie in a 3-inch length of Zonker strip at the bend as a tail.

2. Tie in a tinsel stem and advance the thread to near the eye.

3. Wrap the tinsel stem forward, creating a body. Tie off and cut the tinsel stem with wire cutters.

4. Tie in a wing of white bucktail.

5. Tie in some strips of tinsel as a topping.

6. Make a large head.

7. Apply prism eyes.

8. Cover head and eyes with a heavy coat of 5-minute epoxy.

**MATERIALS**
Hook: Dai-Riki 270, size 6
Thread: Color to match body, 8/0
Eyes: Spirit River Dazle-Eyes, 5/32 black
Tail: Tan rabbit strip
Underbody: Sparkle yarn to match body color
Overbody: Rabbit fur
Rib: Krystal Flash, rainbow

**98**

FOX RIVER RAT
*Tied by Todd Miller*

The River Rat comes from Todd Miller (ToMi_Blkflies@msn.com) of Black Flies in Elburn, Illinois. He fishes the Fox River in Illinois and has hit on a "do everything" pattern for smallmouth bass, carp, catfish, and walleye.

Todd says this pattern works well for a couple of reasons. First, it definitely looks like something alive in the water. The rabbit fur "swims" better than most other materials. In addition, the fly essentially functions as two patterns. It can be fished on a dead drift and bounced along the bottom as a nymph or worked on a tight line with starts and stops like a streamer.

Todd experimented with a variety of colors, but olive, gray, and white seem to work the best. He also likes a white version with a fluorescent orange head.

To get the best results from this fly he recommends casting straight across the current and letting the fly swing. When the line tightens, hold on. If there's no immediate strike, let it swim for a few seconds and then give it a few quick strips. High to moderate water levels seem to be the best conditions for the Fox River Rat. Also, a good current flow is helpful.

## Tying Steps

1. Wrap a short thread base and tie on the eyes.

2. At the middle of the shank, tie in a rabbit strip. Cut the hide at the bend of the hook, but leave the hair as a tail.

3. On top of the tail, tie on three strands of Krystal Flash the same length as the tail. Leave the tag ends long so they can be used as ribbing.

4. Tie in Sparkle Yarn just ahead of the rabbit strip. Wrap back and forth from the end of the strip to the eyes to create a full, but not too thick, body. Tie off in front of the eyes.

5. Wrap Krystal Flash ribbing to the front of the eyes.

6. Take thread back to the tail.

7. Dub rabbit fur; twist tightly. Wrap the overbody to the eye of the hook.

8. Wrap a head.

9. Pick out the dubbing to make a bushy body.

**Materials**
Hook: Mustad 9672, size 12
Thread: Black, 6/0
Weight: Gold cone head
Tail: Black fox fur from the top of the head
Body: Red Ultra Wire
Thorax: Purple Ice Chenille

# 99

## Blackberry
## Ice-Cream Cone
*Tied by Jim Krul*

Jim Krul is strange. It's impossible to know what materials he'll weave into his next creation. I suppose it shouldn't be so surprising, though, because his materials catalog has more unusual stuff than any other I've seen. (Contact him at 845-855-5182 or www.flyfishingu.net to receive a copy.) He's always happy to admit to materials that work, but conveniently forgets about those that fail—you wouldn't believe some of them anyway.

Recently, he's been playing around with fox fur—red, gray, and arctic—and he's discovered that the faces make excellent tying materials, in both natural and dyed. His interest in fox fur actually began years ago when he met a furrier. Jim was looking for the main ingredient for Hendricksons. The furrier suggested he look at the fox heads. They provided a variety of lengths and degrees of coarseness and they were cheap, being a by-product of the fur-coat industry.

A mere 20 years later Jim developed the Blackberry Ice-Cream Cone for small-mouth bass on the Housatonic River in Connecticut. He also claims to have taken trout with it. Jim fishes the fly as a nymph but retrieves it back upstream after the dead drift. Strikes can come on the drift or the retrieve.

So, how did this fly get its name? Black (fox tail), Berry (blue), Ice (chenille), Cone (head). Against my better judgment, I asked if there were other flavors. Turns out there are. For example, the Chocolate Ice-Cream Cone incorporates brown fur, brown Ultra Wire, and root beer Ice Chenille. The Plain Vanilla uses arctic fox, white Ice Chenille, and a silver cone head. If you want an Ice-Cream Cone with a topping, tie in a wing of matching color. Jim also cites pistachio (chartreuse), lemon, orange, and olive as his other favorites.

## Tying Steps

1. Slide a cone head up behind the hook eye.

2. Tie in fox fur as a tail.

3. Tie in Ultra Wire and wind it over the tail butts and forward to form the body.

4. Wrap Ice Chenille to form a short thorax.

5. Tie off behind the cone head.

## Materials

Hook: Mustad straight-eye streamer hook, size 4
Thread: Black monocord, 3/0
Tail Loop: Monofilament, 2 to 4 inches of 20- to
   40-pound
Body: Black yarn, about 10 inches long
Wing: Black, narrow, crosscut Zonker bunny strip
Eyes: Very small nickel dumbbell or hourglass

## 100

Bob's Bed and
Breakfast Leech
*Tied by Bob Rock*

Bob Rock (rwrock@dreamscape.com) of Oswego, New York, first tried this pattern in the famous Great Lakes tributaries. It caught neither trout nor salmon, but did take several smallmouth bass. A few days later the same thing happened, and the light went on in Bob's head. Now he uses this fly whenever he's chasing smallies.

Bob reports that the 3-B Leech is very productive in moving water. He fishes it in the traditional fashion by casting slightly upstream and letting it drift down. He then retrieves it using a variety of speeds from very fast to slow and erratic. No added action is necessary during the drift because the bunny fur moves enticingly on its own. According to Bob, the best feature of this fly is its ability to catch fish through the midday hours, when other flies slow down.

On three separate occasions, experienced flyrodders have told Bob his 3-B Leech caught more and bigger bass than they have ever experienced. As if that weren't proof enough, Bob recently took a 5-pound largemouth with it. Looks like all kinds of bass love Bob's leeches.

## Tying Steps

1. Start a thread base midway down the shank and stop ¼ inch before the hook point.

2. Tie in the monofilament on the far side of the hook shank. Bend it around to the near side to form a small loop that sticks out beyond the bend of the hook. Bind it down well and cement the threads with Super Glue. The loop's purpose is to prevent the wing from getting entangled around the hook.

3. Advance the thread forward to ¼ inch behind the eye.

4. Tie in the yarn.

5. Wrap a body down to where the monofilament sticks out from under the thread and back up. Repeat, if necessary, to form a bulky body.

6. Tie in the bunny fur, hide-side down, leaving room for the next material.

7. Build a small hump of thread and tie in the dumbbell eyes. Figure-eight the thread wraps, whip finish, and cement the head.

**MATERIALS**
Hook: Tiemco TMC 300, size 6
Thread: White monocord
Body/Wing: White, pink, and brown
marabou and Krystal Flash
Eyes: White with black pupil in enamel paint
Head Cement: Sally Hansen Hard As Nails

# 101

## LAKE ONTARIO
## MARABOU STREAMER
*Tied by Bill DeForest*

Lake Ontario is most often thought of as home to heavy runs of large chinook and coho salmon and steelhead, followed by football-shaped browns and the newly reintroduced Atlantic salmon, which have been recorded up to 13 pounds.

However, anglers who live along the shores of this massive lake, and those in the know, try to keep the warmwater species that are present a secret, but Bill DeForest (icedriller123@yahoo.com) of Oswego, New York, is putting the rest of us in the loop. He sent along this bass fly and some instructions on how it should be fished.

The pink color of the fly came from seeing small strips of pink on rainbow fry. In Lake Ontario, the rainbow fry become forage for smallmouth bass and larger trout and salmonids. This is especially true when the fry come close to the shoreline and move into the estuaries from April to August. After all, big fish eat little fish, so clouds of fry are sure to start a commotion. The Krystal Flash and coloration of the Lake Ontario Streamer mean dinner to the predators. An olive marabou version of this fly has also been effective on smallmouths in the Oswego River below the dams and locks as far upstream as Fulton.

In the evenings, Bill likes to search for fish by trolling with a sinking line around and over ledges. Once he finds them he switches over to a floating line and casts traditionally. This method of hunting and casting is productive around river mouths, as well as farther out in the lake.

When the fly is trolled slowly, the black bass of Lake Ontario attack it with gusto. On a recent outing, Bill was guiding and had put down his rod while he attended to the motor. Only his leader was hanging over the gunwale during the repair, but a bass came right alongside the boat and grabbed the streamer. Bill quickly changed the client's fly to the Lake Ontario Streamer, and he caught fish until the fly was totally destroyed.

## Tying Steps

1. Tie in a short thread base.

2. Tie white marabou tips on the underside of the hook, extending to the bend.

3. Tie in six strands of Krystal Flash on each side of the shank. They should be twice as long as the shank.

4. Tie in long white marabou tips on the top of the hook, also double the shank length.

5. Tie in pink marabou tips over the white.

6. Tie in a topping of brown marabou.

7. Build a thread head.

8. Color the top of the head with brown permanent marker and lightly streak the brown marabou.

9. Apply white enamel eyes by dipping the end of a pencil in paint. Let dry.

10. Apply black pupils using the same technique. Let dry.

11. Coat head with Sally Hansen Hard As Nails.

# Index

# Fly Fishing Guide Series

If you would like to order additional copies of this book or our other Wilderness Adventures Press guidebooks, please fill out the order form below or call **1-800-925-3339** or fax **800-390-7558**. Visit our website for a listing of over 2000 sporting books — the largest online: **www.wildadv.com  Mail To:**
  *Wilderness Adventures Press, Inc., 45 Buckskin Road • Belgrade, MT 59714*

☐ **Please send me your quarterly catalog on hunting and fishing books.**

**Ship to:**

Name ————————————————————————————————

Address —————————————————————————————

City ————————————— State ————————————— Zip ————————————

Home Phone ————————————— Work Phone —————————————

**Payment:**  ☐ Check  ☐ Visa  ☐ Mastercard  ☐ Discover  ☐ American Express

Card Number ————————————— Expiration Date —————————————

Signature —————————————————————

| Qty. | Title of Book | Price | Total |
|------|---------------|-------|-------|
| | Flyfisher's Guide to Alaska | $32.95 | |
| | Flyfisher's Guide to Chesapeake Bay | $28.95 | |
| | Flyfisher's Guide to Colorado | $28.95 | |
| | Flyfisher's Guide to the Florida Keys | $28.95 | |
| | Flyfisher's Guide to Freshwater Florida | $28.95 | |
| | Flyfisher's Guide to Idaho | $28.95 | |
| | Flyfisher's Guide to Montana | $26.95 | |
| | Flyfisher's Guide to Michigan | $26.95 | |
| | Flyfisher's Guide to Minnesota | $26.95 | |
| | Flyfisher's Guide to New Mexico | $28.95 | |
| | Flyfisher's Guide to New York | $28.95 | |
| | Flyfisher's Guide to Northern California | $26.95 | |
| | Flyfisher's Guide to Northern New England | $28.95 | |
| | Flyfisher's Guide to Oregon | $28.95 | |
| | Flyfisher's Guide to Pennsylvania | $28.95 | |
| | Flyfisher's Guide to Texas | $28.95 | |
| | Flyfisher's Guide to Utah | $28.95 | |
| | Flyfisher's Guide to Virginia | $28.95 | |
| | Flyfisher's Guide to Washington | $28.95 | |
| | Flyfisher's Guide to Wisconsin | $28.95 | |
| | Flyfisher's Guide to Wyoming | $28.95 | |
| | On the Fly Guide to the Northwest | $26.95 | |
| | On the Fly Guide to the Northern Rockies | $26.95 | |
| | Saltwater Angler's Guide to the Southeast | $26.95 | |
| | Saltwater Angler's Guide to Southern California | $26.95 | |
| | Colorado's Best Fishing Waters | $28.95 | |
| | California's best Fishing Waters | $28.95 | |
| | Field Guide to Fishing Knots | $14.95 | |
| | *Total Order + shipping & handling* | | |

*Shipping and handling: $4.99 for first book,*
*$3.00 per additional book, up to $13.99 maximum*